Black Cockie Press

12 week Novel Writing Masterclass Workbook.

A complete first draft in 12 weeks.

Black Cockie Press

12 week Novel Writing Masterclass Workbook.

A complete first draft in 12 weeks.

Natalie Muller

BLACK COCKIE PRESS

Black Cockie Press

12 week Novel Writing Masterclass Workbook.

A complete first draft in 12 weeks.

Published by Black Cockie Press

Copyright Natalie Muller 2021

Cover design Natalie Muller 2021

Distributed by IngramSpark

Printed by IngramSpark

ISBN: 978-0-6485110-6-9

The moral right of the author has been asserted

Nataional Library of Australia

Cataloguing-in-publication entry:

Muller, Natalie

Black Cockie Press

12 week Novel Writing Masterclass Workbook.

A complete first draft in 12 weeks.

Non Fiction

ISBN: 978-0-6485110-6-9

All rights reserved. Except as permitted under the *Australian Copyright Act of 1968* (for example, a fair dealing for the purpose of study, research, criticism or review), no part of this publication may be reproduced, stored in or introduced into a database and retrieval system or transmitted in any form or any means (electronic, mechanical, photocopying, recording or otherwise) without the prior written permission of both the owner of copyright and the above publishers.

Disclaimer

The material in this publication is of the nature of general commeny only, and does not represent professional advice. It is not intended to provide specific guidance for particular circumstances and it should not be relied on as the basis for any decision to take action or not take action on any matter which it covers. Although the author and publisher have made every effort to ensure that the information in this book was correct at press time, the author and publisher do not assume and hereby disclaim any liability to any party for any loss, damage, or disruption caused by errors or omissions, whether such errors or omissions result from negligence, accident, or any other cause.

CONTENTS

Introduction	6
Week 1 Getting Started	7
Week 2 Finders Keepers	15
Week 3 Character	21
Week 4 Plot	28
Week 5 Genre Fiction	35
Week 6 Literary Fiction	40
Week 7 Literary Theory	47
Week 8 Time	53
Week 9 Experimental Fiction	58
Week 10 Ethics and Self-Care	62
Week 11 Language and Language Techniques	66
Week 12 Seeking Help and Taking Criticism	79
Activities & Templates	87
Index	101

INTRODUCTION

Congratulations, you have purchased Black Cockie Press' 12 week novel writing Masterclass. You have decided to invest in your writing and over the next 12 weeks that is what we will be doing: Writing. The aim of this course is to provide you with the basic tools for you to complete your first draft of 45000 words. That's a big number I know, and you are probably already feeling a little nervous about it, just looking at it. Don't worry, I will be with you guiding your every step. At the bottom of each lesson you will finds a set of Coloured bars mapping out your progress through the course, each week will give you instructions on where in your journey you should be.

So are we ready for an adventure?

WEEK 1 – GETTING STARTED.

Human beings are naturally story telling creatures. Stories are our most direct form of communication, allowing the sharing of thoughts and perceptions of the world from one human to another. We do it all the time, when we ask someone how their day was, when we reflect on our lives, when we explain ourselves to others, we do so in stories. The desire to tell stories however does not translate naturally into the ability to tell a story in print. For this, one needs to learn techniques and skills that creative writers use to create effective writing.

To start one must start at the beginning. In the beginning was an idea. But where did that idea come from? In order to write one must have something to write about, an idea. Attempting to write without an idea and effective planning will result in the terror of the blank page and the belief that one cannot write. The difference between those who write and those who want to write is in their planning. Writers know when to arrive at the page.

Think of it as turning up to work, the writer is the person who arrives at work in a professional manner, they are well groomed, professionally dressed, on time and ready to work. The want-to-be-writer turns up to work unwashed, unkempt and still in their pyjamas. They are not ready for the work ahead of them and as a result, the work will send them home in disgrace.

So what do I have to do to arrive at the work ready to work? You need two things: a writer's journal and an understanding of your writerly identity.

THE WRITER'S JOURNAL

The writer's journal is a very different document than a traditional journal. Where a traditional journal records the private thoughts and feelings of a person, a writer's journal is a repository of ideas, thoughts and observations. It is also a place to explore and experiment with ideas without the pressure that writers can place upon themselves when attempting a complete narrative. The writer's journal is a blank page which makes no demands of the writer. A private space where one can exercise and flex their writing muscles. While each writer is unique and will find their own unique way to use their journal, a few common attributes and

uses of writer's journals can help you find your own best practice.
- Journals are usually small and portable allowing for ease of use. Mobile phones can offer a portable site for notes if your journal is larger.
- Consistent practice is important; this will be good training for once you start writing your creative project. How often you write in your journal is up to you, but weekly writing is considered a bare minimum. Daily writing would be ideal and should be aimed at, this way if you miss a few days it is less trouble to start again, and less likely to be abandoned, than if you miss a few weeks of journaling.
- Your journaling time is also a good way to accustom your family to your writing practices. Selfish as it sounds you do need to give yourself an hour or two at a specific time where you will not be disturbed.
- The content of a writer's journal can include:
    - Titbits, odds and ends. Writers are magpies who gather up scraps of information, conversations and observations which they may or may not later use in their writing.
    - Journal entries do not have to be written, a journal is a great place to paste newspaper articles or clippings as well as recording URL's of interesting websites, and book titles.
    - It is a place for experimentation, especially techniques that you have discovered through your reading. Writers read not only to enjoy fine writing and a good story, they also read to develop their own techniques. A journal is a good place to practice techniques that you admire but are not ready to include in your creative practice yet.
    - Your journal is an invaluable resource for collecting together your research. The interesting juxtapositions of ideas and thoughts that can appear in a journal can make it a fertile ground for new work to develop or new directions to become apparent while working on a project.
    - Worries and crises of confidence. Every writer had doubts about their abilities and whether they are wasting their time. Every writer through the course of their writing life either from external events or from internal doubts will feel blocked and unable to write. This is normal and a writer's journal can provide you with a space to explore these feelings and examine why you feel blocked. Cathartic writing like this can prompt the thought and impulse to begin writing again.
    - Writing exercises are a useful activity to engage with in a journal, especially when you are working to develop your writerly identity or to develop the identity of a character or group of characters.

- A journal can also be a place to reflect on your own practice as a writer. It is a place to examine what it is you want out of your writing and whether your writing is at the quality you are happy with. If not what can you, do to improve your writing? If you are happy with it, a journal can be the place to try experiments which will enhance your existing skills and help you to progress to the next level.

- The journal is also a place to critique the stories and novels you have read. This is especially important if you are interested in publication as reading what is current in journals and magazines will give you a strong idea of what quality, and content editors are looking for in their publications.

• These are just a few ideas of how to use your journal; you will through consistent practice develop your own uses. Remember there is no right or wrong way to use a journal only a right way for you.

DEVELOPING A WRITERLY SELF

• A writer's journal is more than just a platform for practicing techniques and storing ideas, it is a place to develop your writerly self. To do this you have to move beyond what is called First Order Journal Work. This work is private and more reminiscent of a traditional diary, and focuses more on the author's emotional relationship to their writing in an instinctive and non-reflexive manner.

• Developing a writerly self, means engaging in what is called Second Order Journal Work. This work is not just concerned with the moment of writing, but also reflecting, analyzing and taking a critical approach to your writing practice. Journal entries of this order will help you develop not just as a writer of small exercises, but allow you to engage critically with your writing as you work on long projects, such as short stories or novels, which require longer and more involved production periods. This form of writing allows the writer to see writing as an activity consciously and critically engaged with, which in turn helps to demystify the processes of writing and allows the author to see writing as a set of creative skills rather than a mystical impulse subject to the whims of mood and The muse. Reflective practice can help to prevent writer's block, which is often linked to a mystical image of the writing process.

• Developing a writerly self is a slow process accomplished only through practice and reflection. As a result there are no specific activities to encourage this except to say that all the writing that you will undertake in this course will contribute to your development of a writerly self. Writers with a strong writerly identity have developed this over hundreds and thousands of hours of writing practice.

PLANNING TO START.

Why does this course not start with writing immediately? Why are the first three weeks devoted to preparation? Surely, you just sit down and start writing. I know you are thinking this and I will answer you. Writing a book, is not just writing a book. If it were that simple everyone would be able to do it. The biggest myth in writing is that you wait for inspirations to strike and then write out your story in a burst of inspired madness. I'll let you in on a secret, inspiration will give you an idea, but structure and discipline will get the novel finished. If you acquire the skills and deploy them effectively, the reader will not be able to tell the difference between the passages that you wrote while inspired and those you wrote because you had to get your words done for the day. Writers write.

Part of writing means carving out a specific time and place to write. Writing is a complex mental process and cannot realistically be sustained for longer than 3 hours at a stretch, ideally I would say 1 ½ -2 hours is best to shoot for when starting out. You can always extend the time if you feel well in the flow of writing, but don't push. Once you have to push the work ceases to be of a high quality and usually needs to be rewritten before the next day's writing can begin.

The way the writing component of this course is structured is to allow for 5000 words to be written each week for 9 weeks. How you divide these words up across the 7 days is up to you. You may wish to have two short writing periods a day and write 500 words in each, you may wish to write 1000 words a day and have two days off to rest and plan your next move. You may find that you naturally write more than 1000 words a day or that 750 each day is enough for you. Just as I would set a time limit of 3 hours as the maximum time spent writing, I would also suggest that 3000 words would be a good maximum for a single writing session. Professional writers themselves rarely exceed these limits, the thing that makes them different from unpublished or beginner writers is that they are consistent.

A 90,000 word novel can be drafted in 60 days if the writer consistently writes 1500 words a day. Discipline and consistency is the key.

Now the most difficult part of consistent writing is consciously entering flow state. Flow state is a state of mind characterised as an optimal state of consciousness where we feel and perform at our best.

Now entering Flow state takes time and practice, don't be discouraged if you don't experience Flow state often or at all while writing your first draft. You are training your brain to accept this new way of being. There are some tricks that I learnt on the way that can help your brain settle and recognise that you have entered the writing space and that your writerly self, rather than your ego self is required for the duration.

- Music can help – choose music without lyrics, classical or other instrumental music can be useful to help your chatty mind focus while you settle into writing. As I write this I am listening to music. Not because I need it to access Flow, but because it helps entertain me while I write technical works like this. I don't listen to anything when I write novels anymore.
- An oil diffuser incense or scented candles – Our senses of smell are linked strongly to memory, using a scented oil can help jolt your mind into flow state.
- Walking – many creative people throughout history have found walking conducive to formulating ideas or for helping them make the transition into flow state. I do this before writing.
- Writing first thing in the morning – my inner critic doesn't like early mornings, so I find that while she sleeps in, I can knock off 1500 words without her. I got the whole final draft of my novel written between 5:30 and 7am.

You will find what works for you.

PLANNING FOR PROBLEMS

I know we all like to stay positive, but problems are going to arise despite our wishes. It is better to plan for these eventualities and not need your plan, than to panic and seize up because you don't know how to move forward.

MY WORD COUNT IS TOO LOW.

This is a first draft, there is no right or wrong for a first draft word count. I placed the 45000 word count on the task because I find that it is a number that is adequate to providing enough material to build a novel from, as it is half way to a publishers 90,000 words needed for a trade paperback.

However, it is not proscriptive, you may find that you can write more or need less. Though if you are planning on creating a publishable final draft I would not go below 20,000 words as you will not have the material to develop in subsequent drafts.

I AM BLOCKED.

Ah, the dreaded writers block. It doesn't exist. What does exist is anxiety and self-criticism. This combo will work to kill creative work dead in a moment. This is a first draft. No one is going to read it but you. Think of it as a scale model of the final product. It doesn't need to be perfect. Your inner critic is a bitch, hit her with a shovel and bury her beneath the roses. You can dig her up when you are ready to revise and edit.

The other reason people become blocked is because something is not working in the narrative and something in you knows it. You want to plough ahead, but there is a nagging doubt that says it will all derail down the track if this is not fixed. Back track and work out what it is that is bugging you. Trust that your subconscious knows something that you can't see yet. Leaking plumbing doesn't miraculously heal itself just because you brick it over. Fix structural problems when they emerge, it will save you time in the long run.

MY FRIEND/PARTNER/MOTHER WANTS TO READ IT.

Don't let them read it until you are ready. The first draft is you telling yourself a story. You will know when it is time to tell the story to another person. Don't let them pressure you into revealing it too soon.

HOW CAN I CALL MYSELF A WRITER?

Being a writer has nothing to do with being published. You are a writer if you write. I give you permission to call yourself a writer. When you write something, have it published, receive payment, and use the money to pay a bill, you are a professional writer.

STORY STARTERS

The following prompts are for you to use to help you settle into a writing

routine. Choose a new prompt each day and write without critical thought until the thought peters out.
- "I want to preface this by saying nothing happened, nothing is on fire. It is mere speculation. Do we have a fire extinguisher?"
- I couldn't find a dragon on sale.
- The trick is to not let people know how truly weird you are until it's too late for them to back out.
- If you don't terrify people a little bit then what's the point?
- "If we get arrested it's your fault."
- "So you're a human? Like 100% actual human? I've heard scary things about you guys."
- I never believed that they existed, but here was one staring at me.
- "I didn't do anything. I don't know why I'm down here."
- "Use me as a lab rat for your experiments one more time and I won't be responsible for my actions. Understand?"
- "I'm not human. I never was. So why are you expecting me to act like one?"

Week 1

◦ This week is all about settling into the process. Use this week to organise your writing time. Practice flow working using one of the writing prompts each day to establish a rhythm.

WEEK 2 - FINDERS KEEPERS

If you were to ask, what makes the writing of a writer who completes a work different from those writers who endlessly start, but never complete projects, I would say it is research. Research is a topic rarely discussed in creative writing courses or website, and yet it is a most crucial skill in the writing process, without it one is merely performing writing tasks. Writing is not as many people believe, merely a process of 'making things up'. All writing, even the most imaginative fantasy or science fiction, requires research. It is the difference between writing that is flat and un-engaging, writing which engages the reader in a living and recognisable landscape.

'That's all well and good for realist fiction, but I'm writing fantasy!' I hear you say. I reply that the biggest failing of these works is lack of grounding. When a work is surreal or fantastic in nature, the writing requires a greater attention to research to ground the story in some recognisable reality. The alternative is characters which are mere tropes for plot development and a plot which is dull and predictable punctuated by passages meant to be exciting and thrilling, but which are cliché and obvious to readers who are skilled readers of genre. Note readers of genre fiction are unimpressed by writers who take their interest for granted. Readers of general and literary fiction are equally critical of writers who offer little and take their interest for granted.

This neatly brings us to our first topic of research:

READ THE GENRE YOU WISH TO WRITE

I once read the manuscript of a man who wished to write a short story in a romance genre. He wished to do this because he believed that it would be easy, he had never read romantic fiction in his life. His lack of familiarity with the genre showed. His depiction of the heroine was misogynistic and showed contempt for women. His poor attention to plot and character showed his contempt for his female audience and his assumption that they would read any dross so long as it was 'romantic'. The use of a male protagonist who could only be described as a loser, showed how little he understood the genre. Even the most cursory research would have told him that the modern Romance genre was born from three novels,

Wuthering Heights by Emily Bronte, *Jane Eyre* by Charlotte Bronte and *Pride and Prejudice* by Jane Austin, and that heroes in these novels are based upon either Mr Darcy whom as we all know has £10,000 a year and looks like Colin Firth! Or those readers with a more gothic bent know that heroes are dark, brooding and passionate like Heathclif.

So what is the moral of this little tale? If you intend to write genre fiction, be a fan. The majority of genre fiction writers are as much fans of the genre as the readers. They know the genre they are writing in better than the readers do, thus when they break the 'rules' or conventions they are doing so with full knowledge in what they are doing. Editors will reject works that fail to respect the genre and the readership. To avoid a string of rejection letters you need to do the most basic of research and look at the conventions of genre and the style and content of journals and publishers to which you wish to submit your writing. One does not send fan fiction to Meanjin or literary fiction to a science fiction journal.

BUILDING STRONG FOUNDATIONS

Strong writing is built on a strong foundation. Every story regardless of its content will require some form of research. The most basic skill in your research tool bag is Information Gathering. This process may be engaged with at any point in the writing process. Often it is undertaken at the outset of the writing process, where once an idea has been identified the writer will seek out the information needed to fill gaps in their knowledge. The sources of information are many and varied they can include:
- Non-fiction books and academic journals
- Firsthand accounts e.g. letters, diaries, newspaper reports, blogs etc
- Film and radio documentaries and podcasts
- Interviews with experts, professionals or witnesses
- Museums and galleries
- Visits to actual locations
- Photographs, paintings and other visual records.
- Music and songs.

TURNING YOUR RESEARCH INTO STORY

Once you have begun to find the information needed to write your story, you need to work out how you are going to use it. Information is not useful in an unprocessed form, stories which suddenly stop the narrative to give the reader detailed information makes for unbelievably boring reading, no matter how fascinating you find the content. Amassing information in and of itself is not research. Information is only research once it has been digested and used to create new knowledge and understanding about a particular subject. This new knowledge will be express through the originality of a writer's work. You may be writing a story about a murder, but the research that you undertake while writing will show a particular and original knowledge about the crime or humanity. Works which rely on formulaic plots and stock characters do not require research, but nor do they engage the reader. Real research involves reflection, writers consider how they will tell the story they are writing in the light of the information that they discover. They will adapt and experiment with narrative possibilities that the new information may open up.

USING FOUND STORIES

So you have decided to write a novel. You might have an idea that you would like to write, but what if you don't. How do you come up with a compelling story that will hold your attention and be worth telling? Well, let me let you into a little secret. You steal it. You find a lost plot and use that to hang your story on.

NEWSPAPERS

Newspapers are a wonderful resource for finding lost plots. Digitised archives of which there are now many, offer literally tens, if not, hundreds of thousands of potential stories that the novelist can raid. These resources are particularly useful because they are told succinctly, the actors are most likely long dead (and you cannot defame the dead), and they are fairly inexhaustible. You don't need to worry about another writer 'stealing' your idea as they are all public domain, and the nature of newspaper reporting means that if you find a particularly big story, you can follow it as it develops over time, especially big crimes. Some of these can be followed right up to sentencing.

MYTHOLOGY

I can already hear your objections, you don't write in a realist genre, you write fantasy or Science fiction, newspapers are of no use to you. I'm way ahead of you. Another source of free plots is mythology. These stories are the distilled essence of narrative. And what they show us is that we have been telling stories about relationships for millennia. Sure myth has allegorical factors wrapped up as mythic beasts, but at the heart of all of these stories is a relationship. Often they are the story of a young person growing into adulthood. Sometimes they are about overthrowing a great evil. But at their core they are about relationships. This is something to remember, you can have all the imaginative elements you can think of, but if your relationships don't work. Nothing else will.

HISTORY

Now here I am not talking only to the historical novelists. Nor am I talking of big recognisable historical figures, though you can use these if you wish. I'm talking about minor stories that pop up throughout history. The minor players who are caught up in world changing events, or the local stories that make up the collective memory of a community. Even the family stories that are passed down. All of these are fodder for the canny novelist. Just because a story takes place in a particular time and place doesn't mean that you need to anchor it there.

Once you liberate yourself from literal thinking when looking for stories and you will find that there are more stories around you than you have time to write.

I'VE FOUND MY STORY NOW WHAT?

Obviously you can't just write up a whole story based only on a small newspaper column or a family anecdote. So how do you turn it into a story worth telling? I'm glad you asked that, let me take you through the process.

FIND YOUR STORY.

A KATOOMBA SUICIDE.
Bookmaker's Fatal Jump.
SYDNEY. Thursday April 11 1927
When the case of George Williams (45), bookmaker, who had been charged with having at Randwick on March 29th, assaulted Edward Ling, occasioning him actual bodily harm, was mentioned at the Central Court to-day, it was stated that Willams had committed suicide by jumping from Echo Point last Sunday.
(Tearing off his coat and hat and shouting, 'Look after them-' a man said to be Williams jumped from the look-out at Echo Point, and crashed on the rocks 575ft.

below.)

Now that you have a story that sparks your interest. Use the information within to search for more articles on the story to help you flesh it out. Sometimes these stories will only have one story written on them, other times they constitute a whole series of articles that run for weeks or months. In this example it becomes clear that George Williams not only was facing assault charges, he owed money to other more powerful men and this all contributed to his death. There is also an eye witness account of his actual death, apparently he dove off the edge of Echo Point like a high diver.

Who are the characters who will populate this story? Obviously, George Williams, Edward Ling. Mrs Williams is another character, any children they might have. The men George owes money to. The witness. These are a basic list, more characters will present themselves as the story develops.

Now interrogate your story. Bookies are tough men, he would not commit suicide over some assault charges. That means that the men he owed money to are the likely causal factor. What kind of threat was he living under that diving over the cliff was preferable to ending up in their power? Suddenly you have a story that has links to organised crime in Sydney. How did George become involved with such men? What was the gang land scene like in the interwar period of Sydney? Why did George assault Mr Ling, did this have anything to do with the money problems? Had George got himself in deeper than he planned?

Now you need to work out where your found story fits into your novel. This particular story looks like it belongs as a climactic end point. It could be an event that begins the novel and the story works its way back, answering the questions this event raises. Are you going to keep the story in the 1920's or will you set it at a later time or even the modern day? What changes will you have to make to do this? From whose perspective will you tell the story, George Williams? His wife? The police? Whose story is this? Each writer will chose a different path, and each path will allow for a different story.

You are now ready to start planning you novel. Every writer will plan out their novel differently. I don't like heavily structured plans, preferring to pick a destination and then let the story take me there. To this end I use a cork board with file cards that I pin onto it as I develop new plot points or characters. You may like to storyboard it, dot point list it, the choice is yours. Once you have a plan, no matter how basic, you are almost ready to start writing your draft.

Week 2
  ◦ *Follow the process outlined for exploring found stories to develop an outline for your novel.*

WEEK 3 - CHARACTER

No matter what your idea for a story it will need characters. Characters, whether human, alien, fantasy or anthropomorphised animals or plants will be the conduit through which your reader explores your world.

Characters are the first topic to be looked at before anything else, because if you cannot write engaging believable characters then nothing else matters. Without characters, you may as well stop now.

Every reader has their favourite characters that seem to have lives beyond their story and remain with us our whole lives, no matter how long ago we read the book.

CREATING CHARACTERS

Many tools are available to you when it comes to creating characters. These are useful for the initial brainstorming stage. Successful characters will develop along with your story. If your character never develops beyond your original sketch and never challenges you to think differently about them throughout the drafting process then they are ciphers for your own concept of how the character should be and not a character. If this happens, your work will struggle to sustain a reader's interest.

As starting to create a believable person can be hard; the following resources may be of some use.

- Astrology books - many different personality types that can be combined and adapted to suit your needs. Especially when you mix eastern and western astrology.
- Templates - that is adhering to traditional ideals of heroes, villains, etc and the roles they play in the style of story you are telling. Especially useful for plotting a story off mythology or folk tales.
- Using people you know (Not recommended unless you use people you know to create composite characters. Australia's defamation laws are very strict.)
- Lost souls - Pick a picture and get to know them intimately. Activity on pg 87

SPECIFIC RATHER THAN GENERAL

This is a topic that we will be discussing again in a couple of weeks when we talk about setting. Here we are discussing the importance of creating characters that are unique. As I mentioned earlier characters that are general or sketches are dull. It doesn't matter if your intention is to write a society lady in Sydney's eastern suburbs or a miner in Broken Hill, the reader must see them as an actual person. You may think that you know what an Eastern Suburbs socialite is like; you may think you know what a miner from out west is like. I can guarantee that unless you have met either of these people or have experienced this yourself you don't know what their lives are like, just the image of them projected by other writers and television. This is where your research comes in. You need to meet them. If you can't meet them in person because they are historical or inaccessible, find the letters and diaries of people who lived similar lives to your character and read those.

The beauty of this type of research is that most people are perfectly willing to talk about themselves if you are upfront about what you are asking for and you respect their privacy and boundaries. If you need to know what it is like to be for instance a butcher, ask them. Make sure the shop is not busy when you do, you may be surprised how much they are willing to share with you. The same goes for learning any specialised knowledge that they can share to make you story more grounded.

CREATING PERSPECTIVES ON CHARACTERS.

It isn't enough just to create a character, you must also think of how they will be perceived by others. No one is universally liked or hated in this world; even the greatest war criminals have their supporters, so you need to think about how your characters will work when they are placed in situations together.

- How do they see themselves?
- How do others see them?
- How do you see them?
- How do you want the reader to see them?
- What role will they play in the story?

CHARACTER PSYCHOLOGY

One thing connects all the characters in unpublished manuscripts that I have read over the years, the characters are two dimensional. Characters are the readers companions through the story, their lives are what we become emotionally invested in. If the reader cannot connect to your characters then they won't read your novel.

EMPATHY

There are three types of empathy, as a writer you must use the right one to produce the appropriate effect in your reader.
- Cognitive empathy is the ability to intellectually understand the emotional responses of others. This is a cold kind of empathy, even psychopaths have this kind of empathy, allowing them to manipulate their victims.
- Affective empathy is the ability to have a mirrored emotional response to others. Feeling what another is feeling. This is the form of empathy that stops you being a psychopath, but can also lead to burn out in caring professions.
- Empathic concern a combination of the previous two with the addition of action. I understand how you feel, I feel what you feel and I will do something to help alleviate your pain.

As a writer you need to harness your inner psychopath. Storytelling is above all a manipulative exercise, you are seeking a particular response in your readers to fulfil their need for entertainment. The genre of the story or the nature of the events described will dictate the desired response, but your cognitive empathy will provide you with the understanding of how a reader will respond to any given event in the story. You cannot afford to access your affective empathy at this stage of the writing process, it will only cloud your judgement and impair your ability to write the scene. Affective empathy is for the editing process, as you assess the effectiveness of your execution. I know, I just made writers sound like bloodless icy monsters, what can I say? Welcome to the world of professional writers. Seriously though, feeling too much compassion for your characters and protecting them from harm will only compromise your story and make it a boring read.

EMPATHY. NOW WHAT?

Let us return to the two dimensional characters of unpublished manuscripts. What distinguishes them from the three dimensional characters that populate the novels that we know and love? Let's take a detective novel for example, these seem to be very popular amongst unpublished writers. (I think they think they are easy to write.) So the typical detective in an unpublished manuscript, will move through the manuscript fulfilling the role of the detective. He or she will also be infallible because they are the "hero". And hampered by the incompetence of those around them, because they can see three moves ahead and already know who the killer is on page three. Now think of some of the great characters in fiction.

Mr Darcy is more than just a romantic hero, he has characteristics that help or hamper him depending on the situation. He is incredibly introverted and finds it hard to interact with strangers. He uses his social standing to provide cover for this, but it makes his primary role as a romantic hero difficult as he produces a poor first impression and this makes him less attractive to potential marriage partners.

The pleasure of a great character comes precisely because they are not the perfect hero type, yet they hold the protagonists' role and the readers attention. They are richly complex characters with multifaceted lives that interact in different ways with their role in the narrative and provide conflict and interest. When a character does nothing, but move through a plot like a chess piece, they do not come across as people, but as stereotypes.

ARCHETYPES AND HOW TO USE THEM.

Jungian archetypes are powerful storytelling tools. They are ancient, cross cultural and easily recognised. One doesn't need to be a Jungian psychologist to recognise the following archetypes, nor to work out the role they would play in a story:
- The hero
- The maiden
- The tyrant
- The good king
- The crone
- The Great mother
- The temptress
- The trickster

- The mentor
- The monster

These are tropes not actual characters, they have passed down through millennia and been refined through oral transmission, which in a need for economy strips the narrative and character to its essentials. As a result these archetypes are far too clumsy to be transplanted into a narrative and create believable characters.

In fact one of the biggest criticisms of Archetypes is that they are too simplistic for written narrative, what works perfectly well in oral traditions, does not work so well in written narrative, which demands psychological reality. That is not to say that Archetypes are unusable, but they must be digested and flesh retuned to the monumental bones that our ancestors left us. We find archetypical stories satisfying because they are so familiar to us, but a novelist must find a new way to tell such stories and such characters so that they resonate with us in our modern world.

Another big criticism is that the gender roles are too tightly defined and women are allocated only passive roles in the narrative. As a result stories that rely too heavily on archetypes are often criticised for their lack of female characters, or poorly developed female characters.

PSYCHOLOGICAL TRAITS TO REMEMBER.

However you decide to scaffold your character it is important to remember the following when building believable characters for your novel.

- Nobody is perfect, in fact perfect characters are really boring. Flaws are not built into characters just to give them something to overcome, they are there to make them human. Perfect characters are insufferable and unrelateable. Readers don't want perfection, they want human, and humans are falwed. Prince Charming is dull, he is a trope and a trophy, not a real person. Real people mess up and we like them inspite of that.
- Characters have friends, and the nature of their friendships tell us much about them. A man with only shallow relationships is going to be unbearably lonely. A woman whose friends only appear in the story for her to moan about her boyfriend, is going to find herself alone before the end of the novel. If managing a wide social group seems unmanageable for the story you are telling, then give them one but make it clear why they only have one friend. John Watson is the first and only person to find Sherlock Holmes anything other than horribly insufferable. That is why

Sherlock has only one friend.
- People don't follow the most logical actions just because it will help your plot. People procrastinate, they do things against their own interests, and they make horrible messes of their lives. We as humans are constantly fighting against our subconscious desires, and sometimes they win and we do things we know we shouldn't. So too should your characters.
- Your characters personalities must have a logical coherence, ie you don't find many introverted sales people. Or extroverts who work in coding. You do however find a great many introverted performers, they enjoy the act of being someone else. And an extrovert may be happy to work from home, provided their need for social interaction is met in other ways.
- Mental illness is not a character trait. Crippling anxiety or depression or any other mental illness you may wish to use, is not the person. You still need to build a personality for the character and then show how the mental illness impacts their life.
- A character's beliefs must be historically appropriate. This is a big one for historical novelists. It is not possible to espouse post-Enlightenment thinking in a pre-Enlightenment world. You cannot have a character go against tradition and knowledge long before those traditions and knowledge were widely challenged. So your plucky young woman in a plague ridden medieval village, cannot magically have knowledge of medical treatments long before they have been developed. She will be just as superstitious as the rest of the village, unless she wants to be burnt as a witch. FYI she doesn't want to be burnt as a witch.
- Distressing situations emotionally compromise people. Your detective won't be able to continue working on the case involving the murder of his family. Showing him drinking to cope is not providing emotional insight, it is a cliché. Distressing situations change people and that change has to be accommodated as you move forward. Ultimately the trick to creating three dimensional characters is to project yourself empathetically into their place and work out how you would react in that situation, or if their reaction feels authentic.

Week 3

○ Create character profiles for your major characters, using the Lost Souls activity and the Character Building Template.

WEEK 4 - PLOT

The plot is the story the journey that the characters follow throughout the course of the novel. A plot can be complex or simple. It is the basic story line.
What is the difference between a plot and a story?

- Story – simply tells that two events in the same temporal world follow each other. i.e. The King died and then the Queen died. This is the kind of thing one sees in myth, legend and folklore of preliterate societies. Stories are kept simple to aid in the transmitting of them orally. In other words, one event is followed by the next without connection into a larger narrative.
- Picaresque – similar to the basic story, but able to sustain the narrative over a longer period. A picaresque plot follows a cast of characters through a series of adventures or stories, often connected by no more than that they share the same space and time, as in The Decameron or The Canterbury Tales. Early novels often had picaresque plots where the characters move through a series of adventures with little development, but with lots of action or adventure e.g. Tom Jones or Manon Lescaut.
- Narrative – a narrative is the most sophisticated way of telling a story of the three discussed here. In narrative fiction events follow each other just as in the previous examples but there is a great emphasis on the cause of an event and the effect of it. Narrative fiction allows the reader to see why things happen not just watch them happening. It also allows for the story and characters to develop and change from where they started out, something that is denied in the previous two forms. Narrative fiction tricks the reader into believing they are watching independent beings directing their own destinies.

The typical characteristics of a narrative fiction are:

- A degree of artificial fabrication or construction not usually found in spontaneous conversation. Sequence, emphasis and pace are planned ahead.

- A degree of Prefabrication. In other words, narratives often seem to have bits we've seen or heard, or think we have seen or heard, before. I.e. Romance novels. And the kinds of things people do in narratives (not just being born and dying, but falling in love, going on long quests, coming to discover more about themselves or others) seem to repeat themselves over and over again – with important variations of course.

Note: Narrative fiction was developed and written by middle class white men. This had an impact on women, working class and ethnic writers, as the important public and social exploits of these men were not often in the world sphere of other writers. Writers from alternate backgrounds and traditions have had to find ways of using the characteristics of narrative to tell the stories they want to tell, while also being valued as writers and having their voices valued.

- Narratives typically seem to have a 'trajectory'. They usually go somewhere, and are expected to go somewhere with some sort of development and even a resolution or conclusion provided.

- Narratives always have a teller, and that teller, no matter how back grounded, or remote, or invisible, is always important.

- Narratives are richly exploitative of that design feature of language called displacement (the ability of human language to be used to refer to things or events that are removed, in space or time, from either the speaker or the addressee).

How does all this theory relate to us?

Some creative writing teachers tell students not to worry about the plot of their story, as it will become clear as you write. No, it won't, not if you are writing a novel. As you can see, a narrative is much more complex than just telling a story. The size and time taken on a novel does not allow you to improvise. And while you must be open to change, you must have an end point in mind. It might be a road trip, but you have a destination.

Characters need structure to develop fully, just like children. If they don't have any idea where they are supposed to end up, they will sit in the corner and sulk, or meander into incoherence.

Readers like narratives. Look at the popularity of all types of genre fiction. Rambling incoherent narratives are not the ones which sell well with readers. Readers will take bad writing over a lack of plot. Men especially chose substance over style. This is why so few read novels in favour of History or Biography.

Filling a 250-page novel with beautiful prose that is all descriptive padding is never as satisfying as a good story for you as a writer. You will get bored before you finish. And if you get bored, so will you reader.

WHERE DO PLOTS COME FROM?

Plot can be found anywhere. Shakespeare wasn't above stealing and adapting the odd plot for his plays. In fact, it is doubtful how many of his plays are from original ideas; the general consensus is one – *A Midsummer Night's Dream*. And even then, it contains the marriage for Theseus and Hippolyta, which comes from Greek mythology.

So where can we find plots?
- Myth and legend.
- Folktales.
- History and news items.
- Ask your characters. In the process of developing characters, they can begin to tell you what it is that they want to do.

BACK-STORY

The biggest crime against plotting that is committed by inexperienced writers is the way that they use back-story. One can recognise this instantly upon reading the narrative. Characters are trundling along and the reader is feeling their way into the story, when suddenly the narrator dumps a large passage recounting (not narrating. Recounting!) the past five years of the character's life, under the impression that the reader will not understand what is happening in the present without this information.

For the reader it is the end of their interest in the novel, all character's have a past, but the first few pages in recount form is not the place for the reader to discover the character's past.

Back-story, is as we have seen, extremely different in a short story or a novel compared to how they are used in film and television. Books have no flashbacks. I will leave you with a final image to contemplate in understanding back-story. Imagine that you are making a tapestry and each of the colours is a different narrative technique. If back-story is a blue thread and it is all used in the top left hand corner in a messy blob, you will be unable to use it throughout the rest of the image, which will be lesser for the lack.

COMEDY AND TRAGEDY

Comedy and tragedy are the opposite ends of the narrative continuum. The difference between comedy and tragedy is in the placing of the audience's sympathy. High tragedy and high comedy are both heavily

structured, and become less definite as they come closer together and ultimately lap over. The basic questions you must address are:
- What is the order in this society?
- How is that order violated?
- How do the characters respond to the loss of traditional order?
- How is order restored?
- Is the new order at the end of the play something healthy or is it shot through with ironic resonance?

ALL STORIES INVOLVE CONFLICT.

- Typically, the dramatic narrative will open with some sense of a normal society: we see people of all kinds going about their business, and in witnessing this initial state of affairs we quickly ascertain the various ranks of people, the bonds which hold them together, and something about their value system. In other words, we begin with a society, which is held together by shared rules.
- Then, something unusual and often unexpected happens to upset that normality.

The terms comedy and tragedy commonly refer to the ways in which dramatic conflicts are resolved.
- In comedy, the confusion ends when everyone recognises what has been going on, learns from it, forgives, forgets, and re-establishes his or her identity in the smoothly functioning social group (which may return to the original normality or may be setting up a better situation than the one the group started with).
- The ending of a tragedy is quite different. Here the conflict is resolved only with the death of the main character, who usually discovers just before his death that his attempts to control the conflict and make his way through it have simply compounded his difficulties and that, therefore, to a large extent the dire situation he is in is largely of his own making.

A tragic structure can be modified into a comic one.
Examples of tragic novels,
- *Wuthering Heights*: Heathcliff is a creature whose very existence caused chaos and destruction for the Litton's and Earnshaws. Heathcliff and those he has contaminated must go.

Examples of comic novels,
- *Pride and Prejudice*: despite obstacles the prejudiced Elizabeth and the

proud Darcy are able to come together and marry.
Example of Tragi-comic novels:
- Almost anything written by Dickens. A happy ending for all, but the least able to assimilate into the social order. E.g. Bradley Headstone the schoolmaster in Our Mutual Friend.

CONFLICT

What are the three types of conflict?
- Internal conflict – conflict within the character. This can be any kind of problem with which the character must struggle with in order to achieve their desires or to find peace. The resolution doesn't have to be positive for the character, (only therapists want positive outcomes, art lives off grand passion); it can be a struggle to decide to commit a murder, e.g. *Crime and Punishment*.
- Interpersonal conflict – conflict between two or more characters. This is some sort of problem, which must be resolved in order for the story to progress to its natural conclusion. Sometimes these conflicts cannot be resolved peacefully e.g. Heathcliff's hatred of Edgar Litton. At other times they are the result of a misunderstanding and may be resolved to the mutual satisfaction of all involved e.g. Darcy ceasing to stand in the way of Jane's marriage to Bingley.
- External conflict – this is any conflict that is out of the hands of the characters to control, e.g. a war. Alternatively, it can be something that the character has done in the past, which now affects their lives, being in the past they cannot change it, but are forced to deal with the consequences of their actions. This can form the major thrust of the narrative, e.g. *The Meek Girl* by Fyodor Dostoyevsky. The unnamed man reflects on his marriage while he watches over the coffin of his wife, who that morning threw herself out of the window, and tries to understand how and why it happened.
- Environmental conflict – This is an easy one, people against nature and possibly the best example is *Moby Dick* by Herman Melville. Environmental conflict gives the writer a backdrop to foreground other conflicts.
    - How will your characters react to conflict?
    - How can conflict be productive?
    - How can conflict be destructive?

- Blocking – if arguments between characters stop the plot moving you need to rethink their dynamics. All conflict should move the story forward, even if it appears to be moving backwards. Your characters should never get bogged down in pettiness, what is true to life is bad fiction.

ENDINGS

Things to think about with endings:
- Have you resolved everything in all the narrative threads?
- Has the narrative reached its logical conclusion? Or have you rushed to get it finished?
- If your ending is open ended, does it satisfy the reader or make them feel frustrated that it has not been resolved successfully?
- Have you reached the ending you envisioned at the start of the process or has it changed?
- Have you tried more than one ending?

Readers invest a lot of time with a novel, something that is becoming scarce apparently. Was their investment of time worth it? Or are they going to want their time back?

Week 4
  ◦ *0 - 5000 words. Focus on setting your scene and introducing the characters. Who are they? What is their current situation? Are they at all connected to one another?*

WEEK 5 GENRE FICTION

Genre fiction is in my estimation both the most popular form of fiction writing and the least understood by novice writers. When I am working with beginning writers I invariably encounter one of two genres, Fantasy or Crime fiction. The third genre that occurs frequently is Young Adult, though this is often within the Fantasy genre. The writers of the two most frequently occurring genres fall into two categories: Fans of the genre who wish to write what they love to read. These are the people who have the highest probability of success. They already respect and love their chosen genre and have absorbed the 'rules' through their reading. The second group is more challenging, these are the people who have decided that writing genre fiction is easy. They often have contempt for the form and are already counting the bags of money they will earn when their book becomes a best seller. The poor deluded fools.

CHARACTERS ARE YOUR FIRST PRIORITY

This is possibly not the first piece of advice you were expecting when discussing genre fiction. You were thinking that the most important part of a Genre fiction novel is plot, weren't you. No, just like literary fiction, which we will talk about next week, character is what drives your story forward. Character is also the story building element that most writers either neglect or rush in their eagerness to get to the plot. I am here to tell you that plot cannot happen without character. Your characters need to live and they need to be more than their plot devices or stereotypes. Cynical hardboiled detectives, who have no family life, no private life, no life period, belong back in the 1940's with Bogart. These tropes are thoroughly worn out, readers know this, published writers know this, you need to know this and consider how to make your characters engaging. Stephen King, an absolute master of his genre, does a magnificent job of creating engaging and believable characters whose lives are about to go to hell in a hand basket, but don't know it yet. It is part of what makes his book so compelling. So consider who the population of your world is while you work out what is going to happen to them. If you don't, you end up with a cast of characters like those in a certain prequel by Ridley Scott, which shall remain nameless, where they were so obnoxious, awful and one dimensional, that I was gunning for the aliens to kill them all.

AND THEN WHAT HAPPENED?

There is a difference between a story and a narrative. A story is a series of events which follow one another in a chronological order.
Thus:
Jill wakes up one morning, catches a bus to work, the bus breaks down and she is late for work.
This is a story it is a very basic story and one in which Jill is a passive actor, events act on her she has no power over events. Many genre novels I have read from beginner writer have plots which are merely a series of events linked by a protagonist.
Boy A discovers he is the chosen one and go off to defeat the dark lord. Because he is the chosen one he is passive and helpless to resist the calling of destiny that was foretold 1000 years before. And seriously, how many regimes last 1000 years? Most dynasties bicker and kill themselves out in a few generations. Look at the Julio-Claudians in Rome, barely 100 years before they had killed each other out. Even seemingly stable regimes like the British royal family have been volatile over the 1000 years since William the Conqueror invaded. There have been the houses of York and Lancaster, the Tudors, the Stuarts, a brief dalliance with a republic, the Stuarts again, William and Mary period, and then the house of Hanover, each of which brought their own distinct style to the throne. Not to mention the technological and cultural changes that happened in that time, which challenged and confronted the rulers, just as the rulers imposed their own style upon the country.
A narrative is different. A narrative is causally linked and is constantly striving for equilibrium, which events either deteriorate the situation or enhance it. So returning to Jill on the bus.
Jill is a plain clothes detective working on a spate of robberies in the city. Jill's car is in the shop, so she has to catch the bus to work. Jill's bus passes by the city bank were a robbery is in progress. The robbery goes badly wrong and an injured bank robber hijacks the bus.
Are you starting to see how each event is linked to and complicates the next in the sequence, the situation has progressively deteriorated, and the reader will want to know how this situation resolves itself. Complication built on complication helps to build a rich narrative, and finding a new

normal, a new balance is the resolution of the narrative. This is what you need to build in order to create a compelling plot. Don't make it easy for your 'hero' to resolve the problems they face, and remember that big problems often involve solving a myriad of baby problems.

AND GOD CREATED THE WORLD IN 6 DAYS.

Where do your characters live? Genre fiction, especially Science fiction and Fantasy, involve extensive world building. This is generally the part that most writers enjoy, creating a world that is totally different to the world of the every day. Unfortunately this is often where fantasy worlds all start to look a bit samey. It is a world like High Medieval Europe, but there are dragons, and all the people are post-enlightenment thinkers who know the complete history of their world, are secular humanists and herbal tonics work better and faster than modern medicine. Or it is just like the modern world, but some people are magic or have supernatural abilities. These are of course never noticed by humans who are completely oblivious to the magical beasties that share our planet, and are never subjugated by the clearly superior magical people. There are often huge logic holes in these worlds. As a result they are very hard to believe, and in these genres believability is vital. It is also unbelievable when your villain or your ruling class is a monolithically homogenous mass, which shares a common outlook and goal. And they hold this together for generations without change. Are you buying this? Because I come from Australia and we have had a hard time holding onto a single Prime Minster for a full three year term.

World building is important and I know you are excited and want to reveal your newly minted world to the reader in all its glory in a 12 page prologue explaining the history of the world from the moment of creation to the opening of your book with a full genealogy of both the protagonist and antagonist so that we fully understand where the book is coming from. As a reader I can promise you that I will skip the prologue, as well as any pages of long description of the landscape, no matter how lovingly rendered. I will however notice that your character has blue skin, wings and only eats tadpole like creatures that are farmed in ponds out the back of each dwelling house that floats on a vast mashland. What I am trying to say is think smaller. Don't overwhelm the reader with the history of the universe, show me the ordinary details of the world and expand as the story requires. If your protagonist has never left their swamp, then the mountains are going to be just as awe inspiring to her as they are to the reader, introduce geographic, cultural and historical events as they become relevant.

Even genres that are set in the 'real' world require a certain amount of world building, though again, think small, think about the specifics of this world. What colour is the bus your protagonist is sitting on? What style clothes are your characters wearing? Post war Britain or Europe is not awash with people in fabulous new clothes, Post war America on the other hand, a whole other story. These distinctions help to define your world. The world of a novel much like your own world is made up of the mundane daily items that fill our homes and days. Focus on these and go big when the plot requires it, not before.

AND THE BEST PART IS IT'S THE FIRST OF 12 BOOKS!

Kill me now. I know that you love to read book series, I know that they are very popular. But book series are something for people with a publishing history and the confidence of a publisher behind them. I know that you have put a great deal of work into your world building and you don't want to let it go. But please do yourself a favour, for your first novel write a self-contained story. You can always return to the world to tell the second book in the series, but make sure the first novel is self-contained. Selling a single book is hard. Telling the publisher it is the first in a series of novels will not attract them, it will send them screaming for the hills.

A FINAL WORD

Genre fiction like any form of writing has conventions that a writer adheres to and helps to define a text within a particular genre. These conventions are too numerous for a course of this kind to go into individually. However, beyond the conventions there is writing and that is what will ultimately sell your work to a reader. Genre fiction is not the 'easy' option. To do it well requires just as much work as more 'serious' fiction.

Week 5
- *5000 -10000 words. Introduce action now. What is the inciting incident that makes characters act? Introduce your initial problem that makes life worse.*

WEEK 6 LITERARY FICTION

If you are an Australian reading this, then your best chance of being published by an Australian press or to have the potential to win an Australian prize, especially a small one is to write literary fiction. So what is literary fiction? Literary fiction is only understandable as a form when contrasted with its opposite genre fiction:

Genre fiction is read primarily for a thrilling story and to escape reality. Literary fiction is read primarily as a way of examinging our lived reality and our nature as human beings at any given time.

When it comes to Australian literary fiction I have found that the clearest lessons have come from the old Man of Letters, the terrifying Patrick White. Now the following list reflects this bias, the last four points I would argue are particularly Australian. Most of this list is transferable to literary fiction of any culture, and even some of the things that I flag as being deeply Australian may resonate with you and be useable, I will let you use your own judgement in this case.

DO NOT INTRODUCE OBVIOUS PLOT FOR THE FIRST 1/3 TO 1/2 OF THE NOVEL.

This sounds like a very odd piece of advice. Surely plot is an essential part of a novel. If you were writing Genre fiction, then yes plot is a major characteristic of that form of fiction. Literary fiction is a little different, the primary driver of a literary fiction is character and how the characters develop over the course of the novel. As the novel progresses and characters interact with one another and react to the situations that they find themselves in, the plot will emerge. In all honesty this is the biggest act of faith that the writer of literary fiction commits. They trust that as the characters develop the plot and the themes will emerge. These can be then polished in subsequent drafts, but the first draft is about trusting your characters to bring a story to life as they develop.

CHARACTERS NEED INNER LIVES.

Leaping off point one, is that if you are going to hang your novel's fate on the development of characters, then they will require rich inner lives.

Literary fiction doesn't deal in obvious tropes, you don't find characters easily labelled 'hero' or 'villain'. Literary fiction is populated by complex individuals some of who do shit things to others. Your protagonist may have an antagonist, but their conflict is grounded in the real world and has real implications for both characters. Part of this occurs because the reader is able to understand the complexity of the characters and their motivations, providing a level of nuance that is not available to genre writers. Think of it as Black and White verses Shades of Grey. As a literary writer you are aiming for shades of grey, characters who can be ambiguous in their motives or desires. This is part of the reason that the lesson on character psychology came at the beginning of this course.

Besides given that literary fiction is grounded in the real world, how often do you encounter a mortal enemy verses a person who just annoys you? Mortal enemies are for super heroes, most of us mere mortals just have people who tick us off. Most are too self-absorbed to care about spending a life time plotting revenge for some school yard slight.

INTRODUCE ALL THE CHARACTERS SEPARATELY BEFORE THEY INTERACT WITH ONE ANOTHER.

This is another piece of advice that sounds a little odd when you first hear it. Obviously, not all characters need to be introduced separately, but your major players do work better if introduced to the reader separately, before you bring them into contact with one another. This helps the reader work out where their focus should be and allows them to see the character on their own terms. Literary fiction does have a tendency to be far more introspective than Genre fiction and allowing the reader to grow comfortable with the fact that your characters will spend time alone helps to set the tone for the novel. When you start with high action or conflict, you set the reader up to expect this the whole way through. Do not however, use your introduction as a place to dump back story. Rather show your character in a typical moment, introduce what their lives look like before they come into conflict with others or circumstance.

ENVIRONMENT AND OBJECTS BOTH ESTABLISH MOOD AND CHARACTER.

A few years ago I set myself the task of reading Australian literature, which I did for three years. Over the course of my reading the most successful novels, the ones which I found most accessible, most enjoyable, were those which let place influence the characters and plot.

Just because you are working in the "real" word doesn't mean that you can scrimp on "world building". Location in literary fiction is just as important as it is in genre fiction. In fact location can help to define characters and tone. The type of story that can be told in an inner city terrace house is very different to one set in a coastal village. The other benefit of utilising objects and places is that they can act as an objective correlative: the artistic and literary technique of representing or evoking a particular emotion by means of symbols which become indicative of that emotion and are associated with it. Or a thing that stands in for the emotion of the character. This is also a technique that helps the writer avoid falling into the trap of 'telling' rather than 'showing'. When using this technique it is important to allow the object to evolve organically from the writing process, rather than forcing an association.

CRUELTY AND UGLINESS HAVE THEIR PLACE, DON'T BE AFRAID TO USE THEM.

Because you are dealing with a storytelling style that precludes 'heroes' and 'villains' alternatives are needed to create conflict. This can mean ordinary people doing cruel or nasty things to others. Again we come back to the fact that the characters must contain psychological complexity in order for a literary fiction to function. Part of that psychological complexity, can involve delving into the darker parts of a person's nature. People are not universally 'good'. Stories about good people are boring and read as two dimensional. This has in fact led to genre writers creating dark and complex 'heroes' purely because they are more interesting. Literary fiction is a place where readers go to learn more about the human condition. Macbeth fascinates us because he is a good man who does a horrible thing and is driven mad by it. This is the place where the complex and fascinating characters that genre fiction hints at can really come out and play.

THE GROTESQUE IS IN DETAILS: USE IT.

One of the great features of Patrick White's writing is his use of the grotesque. The heightened reality that pushes just that little too far and tips over into 'carnival'. The grotesque is something that is difficult to manage, and should be used sparingly should you choose to use it, but much like the uncanny it can enhance a description beyond regular description. Look at the way the author has taken the image of a furry upper lip and used it to heighten and reinforce the unpleasant nature of its owner. This is also an example of an objective correlative.

"Ah, Mrs Kelly, so good of you to make it," said the patroness, a stout woman of sixty, with a large amount of false hair piled on her head and a moustache furring her upper lip. "We are at this moment starting a mailing campaign."

Dottie moved to the table, picking up a letter, which accused the recipient of being a German sympathizer

"I thought this was a soldiers' support group," said Dottie, proffering the letter.

"Yes, it is," replied the furry lip. "Would you like to address envelopes, or stuff them?"

Dottie dropped the letter on the floor. Challenging the woman to bend down and pick it up.

"How does this support soldiers?"

The furry lip pressed itself against its lower partner, clearly unused to having its authority challenged. A stream of air was released from the nostrils. The lips unclasped and as composed as it was possible for one who is never challenged can manage, said, "We support soldiers by encouraging layabout homebodies to do the right thing and enlist for King and Country. And through rooting out those who would serve to bring down the country from within. Enemy aliens are an invisible danger."

Dottie quickly picking up her children, placed them back in the pram. "I'm so glad to find that out. Thank you, but I think my husband can do without your sort of support."

The furry lip, watching Dottie wheel the pram back out of the room, would have protested Dottie's rudeness, had she not slammed the door behind her with such force it made the windows rattle and the crystal vase fall from its pedestal. Smashing into diamonds against the marble hearth.

"I should have known not to allow an Irish woman to join. Impudent lot the Irish," said the patroness, returning to the table. Moments later, the sound of the front door being slammed shut, made the room jump.

HUMOUR IS VITAL.

Humour is the light to the shade of your more serious story elements. It would be impossible to write as an Australian and not use some humour, even if it is black as pitch.

THE WEATHER IS IMPORTANT.

Urban Australia, has always felt itself insulated from the worst excesses of the Australian environment. Gardens of thirsty exotic ornamentals are planted to replace the hardy natives, structures of steel and glass offer the illusion of permanence, and acres of shimmering rooves protect us from what was here long before any human, black or white set foot on this land. And when we see our gardens dying of drought, or an infinity pool washed loose and lying helpless on a beach like a stranded whale, or watch in horror as bushfire tears through the suburbs, we remember where we are. This does not mean that an Australian story must involve a natural disaster of some kind, such an injunction would be tedious. Rather it manifests itself in more subtle forms in even the most urban of writing. We are a nation preoccupied by weather. When we are not discussing it, we are observing it or else suffering through it. As a result Australian writing has a heightened physicality about it. Characters are not allowed, as they can be in works from other countries, to forget that they live on a physical plain.

While physical descriptions are not a unique trait amongst Australian writers, the pattern of the emphasis on the physicality of characters, I would argue, is. Australian writings reputation for realism, is earned as much from their telling of stories set in the "real" world, as from their grounding of that "real" world in an uncomfortable physical reality.

AUSTRALIA IS VAST AND MAJESTIC: HER LITERATURE SHOULD REFLECT THIS.

What makes Australian writing Australian? The most obvious and facile answer to this question would be that it is set in Australia. But this would make any book set in Australia an Australian novel, rather than a novel set in Australia. While it may seem authentic to foreign readers, to an Australian reader, it reads as poorly modulated as a hammy accent. In short it will try too hard. The other problem of specifying an Australian setting to qualify as Australian writing, disqualifies works set either entirely or partially outside Australia. So while setting is not the defining trait shared by all Australian writing, it has worked its influence on Australian writing in more subtle ways.

Australians accept the myth of homogeny when it comes to discussing our culture, in our rush to sell ourselves to the world we deny any regional variation, a Tasmanian is Australian in the same way that a citizen of Cape York is. While a convenient fiction for the tourism industry, it is not one that our writers support. Different states produce different writing. The differences are subtle, best recognised when viewed as a group, but there none the less. Life in each of the nations' states and territories brings with it its own unique perspective. The Australia that emerges in White, shares more in common with his fellow New South Wales compatriots, than it does with writers from Victoria. The concerns of a writers from Tasmania have very little in common with those from her counterpart in Western Australia. Although all are depictions of Australia, the perspectives of each writer is shaped by where in this nation she is writing from. There is no singular Australia, yet Australia and the culture which developed to adapt to particular circumstances in each region, shapes the perspective of all writers. In other words, like the wild flowers, we have all learnt to adapt to the soil we find ourselves in.

Week 6
   ◦ **10,000 - 15,000** *words. How have your characters actions improved their situation or made it worse? What new obstacles are you going to place in their way?*

WEEK 7 LITERARY THEORY.

"Literary theory, that's just for academics who write books no one reads. Why would I want to learn about literary theory?" That's what you thought when you saw this topic on the list for today. Don't worry I'm not offended. I do however ask you to come to this topic with an open mind. This topic is literary theory digested so that it is useable for any writer, not pure literary theory as found on university campuses. I wouldn't be that cruel. Trust me.

Literary theory is in essence a lens through which a text can be viewed. The type of theory used will inform the focus of the text. The subject matter of the text will point the writer towards the most appropriate theory to apply. If you are using literary theory it is not something that you over lay onto your work after it is produced, but rather something that you build into the text as it is being written, that can then be recognised when it is read.

Not every literary theory is applicable to all texts, and not every text requires the application of a literary theory. However, even genre fiction can be enhanced with judicious application of literary theory to help it rise above cliché or to make it stand out. This week we are going to be looking at some of the most accessible and adaptable literary theories that you might like to consider including in your writing.

MARXIST CRITICISM

Viewing a story through a Marxist lens means viewing a text through the lens of class and power. Marxist theory is very broad and has multiple schools. At its simplest Marxist theory looks at the power relationships between and within classes in society.

Marxist theory allows the writer to examine the following questions
- Whom does it benefit if the work or effort is accepted/successful/believed, etc.?
- What role does the social class of the author play in the type of story they tell?
- Which class does the work claim to represent? Does it have the authority to do this?
- Who's values does it reinforce?
- Who's values does it subvert?

- Do the characters represent the social class of the author and how does this affect their representation?
- How do different classes interact or conflict?

FEMINIST THEORY

Feminist literary theory looks at the relationships between men and women and their roles in society. Feminist literary theory reminds us that the relationship between men and women in society is often unequal and interrogates those particular social constructs that contribute to that inequality. Feminist literary theory reminds us that literary values, conventions and even the production of literature have been historically shaped by men. It invites us to consider writings by women, both new and forgotten and to consider how stories can be changed or retold through a female centric focus.

A good example of this is Jane Austin. Austin's novels offer the reader a female centric view of the world, one where female considerations such as marriage and social standing are given primacy over those of male considerations. The novels are almost exclusively domestic and do not contain a single scene in which two men converse with one another alone. You are about to counter that Jane Austin wrote romances, and how could that be feminist. Actually Jane Austin wrote about marriage and the power making a financially advantageous match had over the lives of women. Take *Pride and Prejudice* for example, Charlotte Lucas in marrying Mr Collins is considered to be a 'winner', though her triumph is remarkably hollow when the reader, through Elizabeth Bennett is given a glimpse of her married life. So too is Lydia, more to be pitied in her match to Wickham than congratulated. These are not happy ever after tales, but cautionary ones told by a woman who could see the social world she lived in for what it truly was, desperate and mercenary.

Feminist theory allows the writer to examine the following questions:
- How is the relationship between men and women portrayed?
- What are the power relationships between men and women?
- How are male and female roles defined?
- What constitutes masculinity and femininity?
- How do characters embody these traits?
- Do characters take on traits from opposite genders? How so? How does this change others' reactions to them?

- What does the work say about women's creativity?

POST-COLONIAL THEORY

Postcolonial literature is the literature by people from formerly colonial countries. It is produced by both the indigenous and non-indigenous peoples of former colonies. Postcolonial theory challenges the narratives of the colonial power and retells the story from a different perspective. Postcolonial literature often, but not always addresses the problems and consequences of the decolonization of a country. It is also a way for formerly colonised people, both indigenous and non-indigenous, to assert an independent identity from the one imposed upon it by the colonial power. Because of the wide range of countries that produce postcolonial literature there is not a singular example of this literature, nor a singular way of producing it. So I will confine myself to Australia for the purposes of this explanation.

Postcolonial theory allows the writer to examine the following questions:

- What does the text reveal about the problematics of post-colonial identity, including the relationship between personal and cultural identity?

- What characters or groups does the work identify as "other"? How are such persons/groups described and treated?

- What does the text reveal about the operations of cultural difference - the ways in which race, religion, class, gender, sexual orientation, cultural beliefs, and customs combine to form individual identity - in shaping our perceptions of ourselves, others, and the world in which we live? And how do these things clash when cultures meet?

- Does the story respond to or comment upon the characters, themes, or assumptions of a colonialist work?

MODERNISM AND POSTMODERNISM

Modernism was a literary movement that emerged after the First World War. It is characterised by a rejection of modernity, in particular urbanisation, changing social relations, urban alienation and some technological advancements. Modernism is difficult to define because of its adherents contradictory stances on various topics. Some modernists were extraordinarily misogynist, while conversely Modernism is the home of writers like Virginia Woolf, a feminist writer. Some modernists, like Ezra Pound were highly attracted to fascism, while others like George Orwell are socialists. Some modernist writers were highly elitist, viewing the working class as dumb animals, while others like Soviet Writer Boris Pasternak wrote for a wide audience.

Attitudes of modernist towards modernity can be broadly divided into the following categories: Glorification, Rejection and Escapism

Modernism in literature is characterised by:
- Refusal of coherent meaning
- Rejection of realism
- Subjectivity
- Split temporalities
- Unstable identity
- Idiosyncratic language
- Experimental forms
- Split identities
- Focus on interiority
- Unreliable narrator

Modern writers give primacy to form. This results in experimentalism, which breaks with 19th century realist conventions. Modernism celebrates unreliable or even split narrators. It often explores the theme of identity, which is more fluid and unstable than in pre-modern literature. It also privileges interiority over exteriority– the stream of consciousness.

Postmodern literature emerged after the Second World War and can be seen as a reaction against modernism. Postmodernism can be seen as a reaction to the human rights abuses and atrocities of the Second World War and the complicity of many Modernists through either silence or active support of fascist regimes and their disregard for human rights. As well as a reaction to the rapidly changing social and political world of the mid to late 20th century, technological advances, decolonisation, the Women's movement, Gay liberation, and Civil Rights movements.

Postmodernism examines the nature of knowledge, both deconstructing established beliefs and purporting new interpretations. Postmodernist texts unlike modernist texts encourage the reader to consider the act of reading and creating meaning, and that a text is jointly written between the 'author' and the 'reader', thus removing the possibility of any final authoritative voice.

Postmodern literature is characterized by:
   Ambivalent stance towards realism
   Split temporalities
   Ironic narrator
   Metafiction
   Historiographic metafiction
   Fragmentation
   Multiple points of view
   Focus on exteriority
   Pastiche
   Irony
   Black humour
   Intertextuality

Postmodern texts are usually written in clear, everyday language even though their structure can be quite complex.
Postmodern texts are also frequently intertextual.
As a writer I am myself a postmodernist. My novel *Poisoning the Nest* is intertextual, running two narratives against each other, it is subversive of dominant cultural narratives by prioritising voices that are frequently neglected in war stories. It also has an ambiguous ending that forces the reader to wonder what it was that they have just read.

Week 7
 ◦ **15,000 - 20,000 words. How is your character coping with the problems they are facing? How are their flaws and weaknesses hindering their progress? What is helping them get through the challenges?**

WEEK 8 TIME

One of the biggest stumbling blocks of writers attempting their first novel is their use of time. This is at its most basic in the over use of "telling" rather than "showing" in a scene. Usually this is a failure of description and an overuse of adjectives and adverbs. However problems with time have many roots and require different solutions.

PACE

'Book' time and 'real' time are two different things. 'Book' time and 'movie' time are also two different things. Unfortunately, the confusion of these things is a common problem among unpublished novelists. Part of this comes from the way in which novice writers compose a story. Novice writer will watch a film of the story in their heads and then narrate it. This narrating leaves the story rushed. The writer attempts to capture the events as they happen, it's like filling a bucket with a sieve. Thus what ends up on the page is events 'told' and rushed, as these writers don't seem to have any rewind facility on the movie they run in their head. More advanced writers think not in images, but words. Although hard to arrive at translating words into images is a lot easier than translating images into words. This is the most basic and common pace problem that I encounter in unpublished manuscripts. The good news is that this is a problem of experience, rather than of technique, and persistence with the craft will help the writer to make the transition from an image driven compositional style to a word driven one.

An interlinked problem is a confusion between 'movie' time and 'book' time. 'Movie' time attempts to mimic 'real' time. Movie scripts are approximately 100 pages long and one page equals one minute of film. Film also allows action and dialogue to occur simultaneously. When this is attempted in a written format, either action or dialogue is jettisoned as the writer attempts to cram 'everything' into a very short space. What these writer fail to understand is that books are a bit more flexible, one can twist and bend around time allowing the reader to see the scene from different perspective or at different speeds. Now this is not without its dangers, head hopping is one of them. Shifting perspective within a scene is very dislocating for a reader. But time is more accordion like than either film or our perception of 'real' life, it can be condensed and expanded at the will of the writer. A scene has to breathe with the reader, to allow them into the action or emotion. An action scene with short direct sentences, one verb one noun, is going to convey more urgency than long sentence with subordinated clauses.

Short sharp sentences, are totally useless in a slow scene, one where engagement with the characters and their emotional state is what is being explored. One does not want to rush such a scene. As a writer it is important to consider not only what you are saying but how you are saying that and how you want the reader to feel.

FLASHBACKS AND FORESHADOWING.

One of the biggest structural mistakes I see writers make is with backstory. It is usually dumped within two or three pages of the story and goes into excruciating detail of events that apparently the reader must know before they start the novel. Because obviously I, the reader, must be told, not shown; told, all the ins and outs of Sally's bitter divorce, before I can possibly read the story the writer is trying to tell. Of course it doesn't occur to such writers that the aftermath of Sally's divorce should have resonances in the story they are telling now. If the back story has no relevance to the story you are currently telling, dump it. We don't need to know. You as a writer need to know it to understand where your character comes from, but the reader probably doesn't. If however Sally once witnessed a murder and this will become a major plot thread, then that is the sort of detail the reader needs to make sense of the subsequent events. Characters without backstory appear dead and flat on the page, however managing time to allow this information to be conveyed effectively is an important skill for the novelist.

ANALEPSIS – FLASHBACK.

This is the narration of story events that occur at a point in the text after later events have been told. Eg *"When Arch was ten and Jack only three, their mother was killed in a railway accident."*

The events of the narrative are primary to the characters, while the past events are subordinate to them, they are narrated to bring greater understanding to the dominant narrative, not to usurp it.

PROLEPSIS - FORESHADOWING

This is less of a problem for beginning writers, as most will not attempt foreshadowing events in their novel for fear of killing the climax. Though hints are often given as to the direction the narrative is taking i.e. Chekov's dictum that a gun introduced in the first act must be used by the third. Prolepsis however, is a useful tool, especially within literary fiction and first person narration, allowing the narrator to reflect on how their understanding of future events may have been false of incomplete, or allude to a future point in the narrative, that from their point as a narrator is already past.

In third person omniscient narration prolepsis can follow a character or event outside the frame of the novel, showing how it develops beyond the immediate events. E.g.

"Years later, when she ever dared to voice it, Dottie would say that it was the rejection letter from the Repatriation Department, declaring Jack's illness hereditary and not the result of the war that was the final straw for him."

Both Analepsis and Prolepsis can be used independently within a paragraph or together depending on the needs of the author. However it is important to think of time slips like this as salt in a dish, a little lends flavour, too much and the dish is ruined.

FREQUENCY

The narration of events within a story has a bearing on the impact of the finished product. The frequency in which an event is referred to. Analeptic events may be referred to one or multiple times across a narrative. And this will in turn signify their import and meaning within the text. Prolepsis events are not or rarely subject to repetition in the same way.

SINGULATIVE

This is the most obvious form of analepsis. An event is narrated once in the text.

REPETITIVE

This is more interesting than the singular event, as it is the same event narrated repeatedly across a text, often in different ways, with additional information, from different characters, different durations and omitting or mentioning different facts. In the previous example of analepsis, the absence of the brother's mother is referenced 17 times, before the full story of her death is told. The result of this repetition is to show how her death has effected the characters at different points and in different ways throughout their lives.

ITERATIVE

This is the telling how one event occurred multiple times across time. It gives a cyclical nature to the activity, suggesting that it has always been thus, allowing for perhaps a dramatic break to the cycle within the narrative. Or when used in prolepsis a continuation of the cycle into the future.

Week 8

○ 20,000 - 25,000 words. What can derail the progress your characters are making? how do they react to a major reversal? Has the initial problem bred baby problems that your characters could not have foreseen? How do they cope?

WEEK 9 EXPERIMENTAL FICTION.

In 1922 James Joyce published his novel *Ulysses*. It is a work that is both a major contribution to literary modernism and a highly experimental novel in its own right. I mention this because this single dense, and innovative novel has continued to provide writers with inspiration for their own writing nearly a century on. This is what great experimental literature can do. Of course the down side of this is that experiments can fail and the result is unreadable books. But experimentation is the evolutionary engine of writing. Until Molly Bloom's eight sentence stream of consciousness tour de force in *Ulysses*, such a concept had not been considered in literature before. While other writers don't exploit the method in quite the same way as Joyce did, their ability to use this technique is indebted to him. Likewise one may not wish to write a whole novel using Free Indirect Discourse as Virginia Woolf did in *Mrs Dalloway*, but still find it a useful technique for blurring the line between narrator and character in an otherwise conventional novel. What I am trying to tell you is that experimental writing should not be daunting or scary, nor should it conjure images of unreadable prose. Rather experimental writing should be a spice to help flavour your writing a lift it out of the ream of the every day.
So here follows some of my favourite experimental writing techniques. Have a look and see what speaks to you. Remember spices are best used when used judiciously, too many and the dish will be spoiled.

SURREALISM

You are probably more familiar with Surrealism in the visual arts, but it has a place in the literary world as well. The most famous use of surrealism is *The Metamorphosis* by Franz Kafka. In this story a young man finds that he has been transformed into a giant cockroach. Impossible as a literal narrative, the transformation illustrates the psychological effect of the young man's estrangement from who he was, his position in society and even his family as a result of no longer being able to participate as he is expected. Surrealism allows a writer to explore psychological states of their characters. And to comment on how certain groups or individuals become estranged from the mainstream. As a writer it is achieved by presenting the world in an abnormal, even an impossible way.

FICTOCRITICISM

This is a very new genre of writing, comprising of a fusion of fiction and non-fiction within the same text. It developed out of the academic Creative Writing courses during the 1990's and is mostly found within academic writing. However, don't allow the relative exclusivity of the origins of this technique dissuade you from using it.

As a novelist interspersing fact with fiction can change the way that your narrative is read. In fact some older texts do this, *Moby Dick* for example is filled with factual accounts of whaling. The thing that marks out a fictocritical work from such a text is the fact that the two texts speak to one another, while the whaling sections of *Moby Dick* can be skipped by the reader wishing to follow narrative only. In a fictocritical text the non-fictional and fictional aspects are interdependent.

HYPERTEXT

This is a technique that I am particularly interested in as a digital publisher. Hypertext allows a text to be linked to itself or other media to create narrative. Narrative can circle back on itself or create branching narratives so that the text cannot be read in a linear fashion. The reason I am interested in this technique is that traditional publishing has worked very hard to eliminate the e-book as a threat to its survival it was deemed to be when it first emerged. E-books now resemble print books and have been ghettoized as the 'cheap' option for self-published writers. As a result the enormous potential for the technology has been allowed to stagnate. We do not know what a true digital narrative should look like yet. I for one would like to find out. This is an experiment I want to be part of. How does one write a book that can only exist in a digital format?

CONSTRAINED WRITING

This is writing wherein a writer imposes constraints on their practice to force them to find creative solutions. The important thing about this style of writing experiment is that the reading experience should not be impaired by the constraint. The writer should be constrained, not the reader. If you find your writing has fallen into lazy habits that have come too comfortable, perhaps some constraints are just what you need to refresh your prose style and move your practice to a higher level.

CUT-UP TECHNIQUE

This technique involving the rearrangement to found texts dates back to the 1920's when it was used by the Dadaists and popularised in the 1950's by William S Burroughs and the Beat poets. Although primarily used as a poetic technique, the novelist can also use this technique as a way of developing or generating ideas. In a similar way to Keats concept of Negative Capability. Allowing oneself to be always open to suggestion, but not striving actively after it. This is a good way of overcoming writers block or an impasse in a narrative. Breaking a text up and allowing it to speak to you rather than imposing meaning upon it.

LITERARY TRANSFORMATIONS

This technique involves using non-literary texts to convey the narrative. This is actually a very old technique, whereby a novel is told through letters or diary entries. Dracula by Bram Stoker is told in this way, through the letters, diaries or newspaper reports written and collected by the characters. While letter writing has died out as a practice in the modern era, people today produce a multiplicity of texts and textual traces, which could form the content of a novel.

At its heart experimentation involves doing something that you haven't done before. And in doing so changing the nature of your writing. If you don't need a new technique then you probably aren't saying anything new. If you are finding your writing bogged down, stuck or stale, perhaps what you need is to shake it up and add a bit of experimental spice.

Week 9
- *25,000 - 30,000 words. Disaster strikes. the worst possible event happens. How can your character turn this around? What reserves or allies can they access. What aspects of their personality come to the fore?*

WEEK 10 ETHICS AND SELF-CARE.

In 2014 I heard Richard Flannigan speak at the Sydney Writers Festival about his then new book set in Changi. Seated in the audience I had intended to ask when the Q&A section started how he had protected himself from the material he was working with in the novel. Listening to his speak it became obvious that not only was my question redundant, but he had done nothing to protect himself from the potential emotional cost of working day in day out on a book about violence and trauma. In fact he seemed to see the psychic fall-out that he experienced as inevitable when dealing with such material. Seated in the audience to me it sounded of a man boasting of fighting a fire without proper equipment, and then scorning the suggestion that his injuries could have been avoided, had he used protective gear, as weak.

Let me tell you another story. I was given a manuscript to critique where in the writer had decided to use their history of sexual abuse as practice writing. The cover note had alluded to the nature of the contents as a 'trigger warning'. Being a naturally curious person, I ignored this thinking: "How bad could it be?" They were willing to share it after all. I am also a trained teacher and mandatory child protection training leaves one in very little doubt as to the nasty things that can befall children. What I read should not be seen outside of therapeutic practice under the supervision of a mental health professional. And this person was expecting me to critique their writing! I could not with clear conscience encourage the writer to continue. The potential damage that this person could do to themselves and others by putting this material in the public domain was too great. I knew this was not the message the writer wished to hear, as I explained that while their intention may have been therapeutic, the results could be re-traumatising for themselves and others. While I did not doubt the good intentions of the writer, they had given insufficient thought as to the ethics of their writing, both for themselves and others.

Why have I told these stories? Because writing is not a neutral activity. It is an act of communication and as a writer you are responsible for what you say. You are also responsible for taking care of yourself. Listening to Flannigan speak, other members of the audience seemed to react as if the emotional toll of writing was to be expected and encouraged, if it doesn't hurt you must be doing something wrong. I take a different approach, somewhat similar to weight training which I also do. In writing much like weight training if it hurts, you have probably done something wrong and caused an injury. Writing is hard, but it is not meant to damage you.

Sometimes you can have the opposite problem, your ethics of care being deployed you're your characters and wishing to keep them from harm, thus limiting the potential of the narrative. Characters do need to feel the full weight of their own stupid actions sometimes you cannot continually 'rescue' them.

My own personal ethics of self-care mean that there are some things that I will not write. These are my lines in the sand:

- Graphic torture – I don't think that I would write a story which would go here.
- Violence against children especially sexual violence, I don't want to read this and I certainly don't want to write it.
- Maiming characters – Although I am happy to kill characters, I don't like to maim them. Because a) it's disgusting, b) women writers who maim male characters, like Charlotte Bronte in *Jane Eyre*, really seem to have deep seated Freudian issues with men and castration fantasies, not something I would like associated with me. And c) did I mention that it is disgusting!
- Violence against animals – I really cannot stomach violence against animals. I might add that I have been a meat eater and I wear leather, but I place the same rules around killing animals as I do around killing people in my work. It has to be relevant to the plot, and it should not be revelled in.
- Lastly, I am very careful about the way I depict women. I want them seen as whole characters and not as objects. This is something I find particularly important in representing sex. I try to write women who have power and subjectivity, not ones who are only desirable objects.

CULTURAL APPROPRIATION

I don't think we can talk of ethics without talking about cultural appropriation. Cultural appropriation is a poorly understood, and widely argued concept which should be considered in any discussion of ethics and writing. Cultural appropriation does not mean that you cannot write characters from a perspective different to one's own. Such a restriction would be stultifying. Nor does it mean that you cannot include characters who are racially different to oneself. To write in modern Australia and create an all-white cast of characters would be anachronistic at best. Objectors to cultural appropriation are not asking white writers to return to the whitewashed, heteronormative literature of the past. What it does mean however, is that when writing characters from a very different culture or perspective a writer must do their research. They must also think about how their writing may be read by others.

On the whole writing that I have read which would fall foul of critics of cultural appropriation, is first and foremost bad writing. It is writing that is under researched, and relies on stereotypes and clichés. It is the 'gay' character whose whole 'character' consists of simpering and flouncing so that we all know that he is gay. He has no significant partner, no personal relationships, no actual character he is all surface and parody. It is an Aboriginal character who wears a name tag around his neck when the white children do not. It is when a character is written as a helpless drunk based on their Irish ancestry alone. (These are all real examples from works I have read.)

It is not, however, including a character from a minority, be it race, culture, sexual orientation as a fully formed integral participant of the story.

Let me put it this way, it is cultural appropriation for Joe Blogs a white writer from inner city Sydney to write a novel set in a remote Aboriginal community in Arnhem land. It is not cultural appropriation for the same Joe Blogs to write a novel set in inner city Sydney, which includes characters who are Aboriginal.

Ultimately ethics are in place to help us act empathetically with ourselves and others. It asks us as writers to consider the possible hurt that our writing could do, and to work to mitigate that potential harm. It involves considering whether the story we intend to tell is in fact ours to tell, or whether there are others better qualified to talk for a particular community.

Week 10

- 30,000 - 35,000 words. Having faced the worst how is your character going to come back from the brink? What is their plan to escape their problems? How does this change the character and allow them to grow in ways that they could not have forseen at the begining of the novel?

WEEK 11 LANGUAGE AND LANGUAGE TECHNIQUES

There was an interesting experiment done out of Stanford University involving writers. The researchers wanted to discover what made writer's brains different to amateur writers. So they put amateur writers and 3rd year writing students through an MRI machine and told them to develop a story. What was interesting were that the two sets of writers, one who wrote without training and the other who were in the third year of an intensive writing degree showed very different brain activity. For amateur writers the MRI showed intense activity in their visual cortex and minimal activity in the language part of their brains. For the more experienced writers the results were the opposite, intense language activity and minimal visual activity. I tell this story to writers to help explain to them why their writing is not working as they expect it to. In fact it takes me about a paragraph to spot a writer who is still in the early stages of development. Such writers are astonished when I suggest that when they write they run a movie in their heads and then narrate it. I look like a mind reader. I'm not, but I am on the other side of this process and think in words. A result of my having invested the requisite 10,000 hours required to become proficient at anything. So with that in mind, let us discuss words.

One of the biggest stumbling blocks that I find as an editor when looking at a new writer's work, is that while they may have invested a great deal of time and effort into their plotting and character development. They have not put the same care into the words they have used to build their story with. It is like making a haut couture dress and stapling it together. It doesn't matter that you have used the finest silks and furs that money can buy if you use a stapler to put the dress together, in fact it is an insult to the aspects of the writing that are so good. Such writers hope that the reader will overlook the shoddy construction in order to get at the story within, the same way that you will watch a bad film if it includes your favourite actor. But even a bad film generally has the grammar of film correct. Worse still are those who insist that the work be read because it is "true". "It is true, it is true, it is true!" they say. To which I reply, "But I can't read it!" Readability is more than correct spelling and punctuation. It takes more to write readable prose than running a spell check over your manuscript before you submit to publishers. So what does make for a good reading experience?

KILL THE ADVERBS AND ADJECTIVES.

One of the biggest culprits that lure the unsuspecting writer to the depths of unreadability is relying on telling rather than showing the reader what is happening. The unsuspecting writer is traveling along the great ocean of narrative when they hear a sweet sound, the lure of the adjective and adverb. These two modifiers make the task of putting one word in front of another so easy. The words flow out of you. The story rushes on at an astounding pace. No longer do you have to think of how to convey to the reader the full emotional turmoil of your character, you can cinematically describe her as replying tearfully. And the reader will surely see the tears welling up in her soft brown eyes and there will be an automatic understanding that she is struggling to contain her fear and anger at not being believed. In fact there is no need to even mention that your characters have bodies or a physical presence at all as modifiers begin to replace even the smallest of actions. No need to write out in full that:
Vic's long strides devoured the space between them. Eric too was on his feet now. Without a word, Vic's big, ink stained fist smashed into his left eye socket. Eric's eyes began to water, as he pressed his hands against his face.
When:
Vic walked quickly over to Eric and punched him very hard in the face; will do and takes so much less time to write.
The story is racing along now, the images in your head coming thick and fast, so fast that you can barely keep up. Your narrative is coming to its natural ending point, but your word count is hovering around 40,000 words and won't budge. Perhaps I can add more narrative and plot points? Does it need a new character? How do writers get to 90,000 words? It's impossible! I can't write. This is too hard. I quit! You have found yourself wrecked on the island of those wicked sirens; the Adjectives and Adverbs.
So, what is a writer to do?
Kill them.
Kill them all. Adjectives and in particular Adverbs are the enemy of good writing. I know, I know, the words of your primary school teacher are ringing in your ears telling you that these are good words to use when writing a story. In fact they probably marked you down when you didn't

use them and so they became habitual. Here is the cruel truth: You can no more write a novel with high school English than you can do quantum physics with high school maths. It is foundational, it is important to have, but you need to move beyond it to write a novel worth reading.

STRONG VERBS AND NOUNS

Adverbs and Adjectives are generally found in writing where the writer has failed to use a strong enough Verb or Noun. The English language is rich with verbs, and if you find yourself modifying your chosen verb for clarity sake, then you have chosen a weak verb. You cannot make a suspension bridge out of breadsticks no matter how many adverbs and 'very's you add to them. Use the right tool for the right job. Using the correct verb will give your writing elegance, economy and clarity, which as writers is after all what we are aiming for.

Compare the two phrases:

He was so very tired. He could hardly keep his eyes open.

He was exhausted. His head drooped and his eyes closed.

Which phrase gives you the stronger image? The difference in word count between them is one word, but the imagery of the second is vivid and alive, the reader is being shown and thus engaged, rather than being told.

Adjectives are a slightly different matter. Look again at the two phrases, the second sentence of both uses modifiers to create the image. The first is quite weak, caused by the adverb hardly being used to modify the verb keep. As a general rule I remove all words that end in –ly, as they are more often than not redundant or else signal that the verb is too weak. In the second both nouns head and eyes are augmented with the adjectives drooped and closed. Because there are no stronger nouns for head or eyes, the use of the adjective in this context is entirely appropriate. There may be a better way to describe the bodily behaviour of an exhausted person, but it would be overly wordy and distracting. This is an entirely appropriate use of "telling" in a scene. Adjectives allow you as a writer to "tell". Telling is an economical way to convey information to the reader that you don't expect them to emotionally engage with. However, it is very easy to fall into the trap of "Telling" an entire story, which is why I am advising you to kill the adjectives. Less is more, when it comes to adjectives. They are seasoning, not a core ingredient and can always be added in later should more be needed.

Here is another example:
He gave her a pretty bunch of flowers.
He gave her a dozen long stem roses.
He gave her daffodils from his mother's garden.
He gave her a bunch of service station flowers.
The first example is weak. Pretty flowers tells the reader little about the exchange or the relationship between the giver and receiver.
The second example, a dozen long stem roses, brings with it connotations of romance, expense, a special occasion. Is this an anniversary? A proposal? A birthday?
The third perhaps a child giving flowers to his mother, a teenager picking flowers for their girlfriend or boyfriend? It also gives us a time of year, early spring.
The third example, the giver is certainly in the doghouse or expects to be and is trying to ameliorate the anger he expects to be greeted with using a bunch of tatty flowers.
Strong nouns bring connotations and meaning that piling on adjectives cannot hope to equal.
A final word on "Show don't Tell" as a piece of advice. Show emotion, so that your reader can engage with your character and the events described. Tell feeling. It is a balancing act, too much of either will create something difficult for the reader to stick with. The key is learning how to balance them, and that unfortunately only comes with experience.

PASSIVE VOICE. DON'T JUST LIE THERE.

Another block to good writing is slips into passive voice. This occurs when the verb acts on the object in the sentence while leaving the subject out. Grammatically passive voice is correct, but it can be very boring to read. Let us take our previous example of Eric being punched.
Even the poorly written example of: *Vic walked quickly over to Eric and punched him very hard in the face* is an example of active voice.
Vic is explicitly mentioned as the subject of the sentence, he is the one throwing punches. Eric is the receiver of the action, the object of the sentence. Now I will translate the sentence into passive voice: *Eric was punched in the face.* There is no longer an actor in this sentence. The reader cannot see who is doing the punching and the sentence loses a great deal of its dramatic intensity. No longer is it an argument between Vic and Eric,

but Eric is a passive receiver of a punch. The act is still violent, but the intensity is lost.

Passive voice also slips in when conjugating verbs with the auxiliary verb, to be. That is am, is, are, was, were, be, being, had, been.

I won't bore you with an extended grammar lesson, the internet is full of guides to help you understand the mechanics of passive voice, but be aware if you find yourself over using these verbs. It may be worth rereading your writing and considering if there is a more direct and engaging way to say what you have written.

METAPHORS AND SIMILES, NOT JUST FOR POETRY.

When people think of metaphors and similes they think poetry. When people think of poetry, they remember dissecting innocent poems in their high school English class. Great crimes against language have been committed in such classes, not the least being the alienation of most readers from the beauty of language in the name of marking criteria.

Metaphors and Similes are a building block of imagery, see what I did there? Building block is a metaphor. It is impossible to speak a language without engaging in the use of metaphor or simile. When a writer considers the possibility of using language devices traditionally associated with poetry, in prose they find that they have unlocked a far richer trove of language than they had hitherto considered using.

Consider:

It was not the most convenient spot for what he had in mind, not with all the sightseers flocking around the viewing platform like a noisy gaggle of geese.

Now remove the simile:

It was not the most convenient spot for what he had in mind, not with all the sightseers flocking around the viewing platform pointing and exclaiming.

The meaning is the same, but the imagery of the first example is more vivid, more alive with meaning. The reader can understand how noisy and intrusive the tourists are to the man when likened to a flock of geese, compared to when just described as gesturing and making noise. The gaggle of geese also complements the choice of verb flocking, which has already brought to mind an avian image.

Or again, a metaphor this time:

Sitting in the back of his cab, Archibald Kelly was grateful for the elasticity of his conscience. Not that he had been in danger of stretching it out of shape in the past

few years, but knowing of its elastic proportions was of use at, times like this.
Here conscience is likened to elastic, the image painted is a cheeky nod to the fact that the character is a bit of a rogue, a larrikin figure. Not a bad man, but one whose actions push against the tight frame of polite society, without ever breaking through. To express all that in straight description would be not only ponderous, but also far less effective.

Other devices traditionally thought of as belonging to poetry, like allegory, symbolism, analogy etc. are also worth examining as having potential for use in prose writing. Do not make the mistake of assuming that literary techniques cannot be adapted across forms. Except rhyme, that belongs solely in the domain of poetry. Rhyming prose is an oxymoron.

DIALOGUE

Just as our own speech is a way for us to communicate what is happening in our heads to other people, dialogue allows characters to do the same with each other. The difference is that in real life we do not have a narrator who can eaves drop on our private thoughts and relate them to a third party, the reader.

All stories have some form of dialogue, even if it is not verbal. Even a story where a character interacts with no one but her own thoughts will be engaging in an internal dialogue. Dialogue does not have to consist of a back and forth exchange between characters it can include silences and body language.

"Hello," he said, lifting the receiver to his ear.
He could not stifle the sigh that escaped him as the voice on the end of the phone identified herself in the bright, yet firm tones of a professional's receptionist.
"Ah, yes...I've been meaning to call you. About my appointment tomorrow, I have to cancel." He paused, gathering his strength for the question he knew would follow this statement. "No, I don't want to make another appointment."
In the silence on the other end of the line, he could see the receptionist clamping her hand over the receiver and whispering hastily to her superior.
"Hello, yes I am aware that it is a condition of my release that I attend all appointments... No I don't want to go back there... I just can't see that person again."
Silence again, he knows the manager's hand is clamped over the receiver as she searches her computer. Then without warning the hold muzak, an aural assault as usual, though with pretensions of sophistication and elegance in the tinny Chopin.

"Yes. I'm still here... Yes, I would be happy to see Doctor Rosenthal. Thursday, at eleven thirty. Thank you."

If this were the opening of a story, you would probably keep reading. The dialogue has introduced a character, a situation and a conflict. We do not know who the man is or what his appointment is about, or what his problem is with his usual consultant. These questions now raised would be the content of the story.

Now contrast this with a typical beginner dialogue of the same scene.

"Hello, how can I help you?" said the man, lifting the receiver.

"Is this James Blake? I'm from Doctor Hodgin's office confirming your 4pm appointment tomorrow," chirped the receptionist.

"I've been meaning to call you I want to cancel the appointment."

"When would you like to make another?" asks the perky receptionist.

"I don't want to make another, I think I have had enough therapy."

"Hello, I am the practice manager, you are aware Mr Blake that you are legally required to attend all appointments until the doctor signs you off. If you don't you will go straight back to the psychiatric locked ward"

"I know my obligations damn it. I can't see him again, he knows my ex-wife and has been feeding her information about me to use against me to stop me seeing my kids," he growled angrily.

"I can fit you in tomorrow with Doctor Rosenthal," said the manager haughtily.

"Thank you."

As you can see the second version has much more information, but it also blows the whole story. The characters tell each other information that they both know and that the reader should not know i.e. why the man is attending these appointments. It also gives us very little character description for our protagonist. The use of adverbs to define the speech rather than enhance it limits the way that the speech can be interpreted, as does the very factual and unnatural nature of the conversation. Finally, the use of words to tag speech other than 'said' is distracting and adds little to our understanding of the scene.

WHAT IS DIALOGUE FOR

- Dialogue is an action scene, as a result you want to increase the dramatic tension not diffuse it by giving away more than you need to.
- It is a place to show character and the relationship between characters.
- Silence and body language are part of dialogue. Refusing to reply or making a gesture can be as much a reply as making a negative statement.

- Dialogue moves the story forward, but it should not be expositional and explain the plot.
- If you can show the same thing through description of a scene in the narration do not use dialogue to show it again. E.g. describing a beautiful sunset and then having a character describe it a second time. Or having the character speak to set the scene, this usually results in dialogue which looks like this:

"Here we are at the park for our picnic, the sun is shining and the recent rain has made the plants looks so lush," said Jean, spreading the blanket on the grass.
"Yes, though the grounds keeper should cut back the shrubs from the paths the legs of my trousers are all wet," sighed Toby.

ONE LITTLE WORD

The only tag that should be used when writing dialogue is *said*, underlined bold and italicised in red for emphasis. The word, said, is not as some believe boring or dull, it is invisible, the same way that conjunctions, prepositions and pronouns are invisible. When a writer uses a word other than said, they are drawing attention to the fact that they are trying to be original. This is not the place to be original. Use 'said' and describe how the person speaks. To do otherwise is to squander your opportunity to communicate your story effectively. It is also possible to write some passages without tags or minimal tags substituting action from the character in their place. The tags whispered and shouted may be used sparingly.

LANGUAGE CHOICES

Choice of language influences the reader. As a writer you need to think of the language choices not only of your narrator, but also of your characters. Language choices tell the reader as much about the character as the information they convey with those words.
- What does the language of the character tell us about them?
- What do the narrator's language choices say about the characters or situations and the way you want them to be viewed?
- Very important, never write accents or dialects. They never work the way you are hoping they will, either sounding like a culturally insensitive

jab or just incomprehensible dialogue. Convey a character's difficulty in communicating with other characters through their reactions to them, not by making their words unintelligible to the reader.

PERSPECTIVE

Sometimes when writing we find that the story has stopped working or that we have ground to a halt and feel blocked. A good way to help break out of a blocked or stuck piece of writing can be to change the perspective of the scene or whole story. Perhaps the story was being told too directly and a more oblique perspective on the events may provide the effect you are after. Next time you are blocked or stuck consider the following questions:
- How does seeing the story from different character's perspectives help you to understand each character better?
- What extra information do you gain from seeing different character's sides of the story?

Perspective is always very important. Keeping it in mind can help you to realise the strengths and weakness in a scene.
- How do you think you can use perspective in your writing?
- Do you think it could help overcome mental blocks?
- How may your chosen perspective hinder your purpose?

FOCALISATION

1st person narration:

The main protagonist is also the narrator or is a witness to the events related or the keeper of a story, which bears some relation to them e.g. a family history. This places the reader in the centre of the story being related. 1st person narratives can be told as recent events like a witness statement or in the distant past as the narrator retells the story from their past.

2nd person narration:

This is rarely used and addresses the reader as 'you'. This is not an ideal narrator choice for a beginning writer. It could be argued that it is not a wise choice for any writer as it is used so rarely.

3rd person narration:

In 3rd person narration the narrator takes no part in the story, but is rather an unseen force, which directs the action of the characters. 3rd person narration places the writer into a god-like position. Unlike 1st and 2nd person narratives, the 3rd person narrator is able to see everything. Because of this the narrator must appear invisible and unbiased. An opinionated, petty, or cruel, god-like narrator can seem rather unsettling to readers.

3rd person narration is further split into close 3rd person, where in the narrator follows only one character through the story and has no access to the minds of other characters. It is a sort of hybrid between 1st and 3rd person narration. This style of narrator is common in general fiction especially fiction aimed at a primarily female audience i.e. Chick-lit.

ADVANTAGES

1st person narration is intimate and provides the reader with a feeling of authenticity.

1st person narration forces the reader to take sides and follow the story with the main protagonists, you feel as if you are there and one of the group.

1st person narration provides intimate details of the thoughts and feelings of the main protagonist.

1st person narrators can be biased and untrustworthy.

3rd person narration allows the reader to step back from the events being narrated; this can be helpful when the events are of a disturbing or challenging nature.

3rd person narration allows the reader to see things that are happening to and being felt by all characters. You meet them on their own terms.

3rd person narratives are the easiest to maintain.

DISADVANTAGES

1st person narrative does not allow you to kill your main protagonist. They have to tell the story.

1st person narration doesn't allow you to meet the other characters on their own terms, only through the eyes of the narrator.

1st person narrative cannot show things that the narrator was not present at, thus limiting information for the reader.

1st person narrators need a very strong identity which cannot be abandoned half way through the narrative, it can be very hard to maintain 'I' as a character and not laps into self.

3rd person narrative forces you to be a stage manager; you may take no part in the narrative itself. All you do is set the scene, dress the characters, make sure they know their lines and don't miss their cues, or fall over the props. You must not under any circumstances take sides, be mean, pretty or trivial. People generally feel uncomfortable when 'God' is petty and cruel. You must maintain your neutrality.

RELIABILITY OF NARRATORS

1st person narrators are never reliable objective observers of events. They will always be trying to justify their position in the story. Questions you must ask are:
- Why are they telling the story?
- What part is the narrator playing in the story?
- Are they eyewitnesses to the events they are retelling or have they got it second hand?
- Do they have a reason to like or dislike any other character in the story and does this have an impact on the way they are telling the story?

DISCOURSE

What is discourse? Discourse refers to the way that speech is presented in narrative. All words in the narrative are spoken by someone, either the characters themselves or by the narrator. The narrator and characters have a voice that is distinctly different to you as a person.

There are three different types of discourse available to you as a writer. Direct, indirect and free indirect.

DIRECT DISCOURSE

- Possibly the simplest and most obvious kind of discourse, direct discourse is quoted speech. This is the language of your characters. Each character, as we discussed, will have their own voice and style of speech. This includes thoughts, e.g. *"I love Mary,"* thought Fred. *"So why can't I tell her?"*

INDIRECT DISCOURSE:

- Indirect discourse is the voice of your narrator. This tells us who is speaking, what they are doing and where they are. This is the language you use to set the scene and to contain the characters speech. Depending on your narrator this voice will belong to either a protagonist or an invisible narrator. This will have an impact on the language of indirect discourse, but not its function. E.g. *Fred knew he loved Mary, but that he felt he could not tell her.*

FREE INDIRECT DISCOURSE:

- This is a mode of writing, which makes up for the seeming sterility of 3rd person narration. Free indirect discourse allows you to meld the narrator's voice with the characters creating a hybrid of the two. Free indirect discourse allows the reader to view a situation through the eyes of a character. Basically, it is like being in their head. E.g. *Once again Fred thought of how much he loved Mary and still he couldn't see how to tell her.*

Week 11
 ◦ *35,000 - 40,000 words. The climax, it is now or never for your character to overcome their problems. The story is again moving towards establishing a new normal. Your character has grown and must either meet the challenge or fail.*

WEEK 12 SEEKING HELP AND TAKING CRITICISM

Congratulations you have made it to week 12. You should be very proud of yourself. Before you should be a nearly complete first draft of 45000 words.

So where do you go from here? Obviously, you fix up your spelling and grammar and send it to a publisher, right? Yes, if you want them to laugh at you. No serious writer would think to send a first draft to a publisher, but plenty of unpublished writers do this. Don't be one of these writers.

So what do you do?

You congratulate yourself for your hard work. You print out your manuscript, because it is easier to do this with pages in front of you and it is harder to delete the whole file in a fit of self-loathing when looking at printed pages. If this sounds like something you might do, back up your novel and give the drive to a trusted loved one who will keep it for you and not allow you to self-sabotage. What you are looking for in your draft isn't greatness, all first drafts are trash. Also important to remember, your self-worth is not reliant on you writing flawless prose. The prose that you are comparing your first draft to, that novel on your bedside table, has been through multiple drafts, multiple beta readers, and multiple rounds of editing. Writing a book is like climbing Everest, you can't do it without support. Your first draft is the equivalent of climbing Ruined Castle, (a day walk) woefully under equipped, poorly shod, with insufficient sandwiches and water and a little folding umbrella and failing miserably. Of course it looks awful, that's just how it is. What you are looking for are the nuggets of gold that spark your imagination and show you the direction of your second draft.

DRAFTING AND EDITING

Editing and drafting, these are words which seem to say the same thing, more work. However, when we talk about these things we mean different processes and if we don't understand this we can come at a work at crossed purposes.

DRAFTING

This sounds like something your teacher expected you to do, except she meant that you fixed your spelling and punctuation and wrote it out neatly in your best handwriting.

What drafting actually does is allow you to take your idea which you have written out to fill 20 - 40 thousand words and build it into a novel sized work of 80 - 90 thousand words. It is where you take your paragraph sized idea and work it into a short story or poem. This is also an ongoing process, new drafts are created throughout the editing process as new ideas and criticisms are incorporated. A publishable novel may go through multiple drafts or variations until the writer is satisfied with it.

EDITING

Most people think editing is fixing your spelling, punctuation and grammar, which it is, in a line edit. But editing is far more than that; it is about developing the structure of the story, developing the story itself and gaining critical feedback from others.

It is also about a frame of mind, one where you are willing to admit that the work isn't perfect and that you need to work with yourself and others to get it there. This is the process whereby you look holistically at the work and begin to work out why the story still doesn't match the one you first conceived of. It is also where you begin to tighten up the writing, changing paragraphs into scenes, developing character and character arcs through dialogue and action, removing back story and working it into the text rather than just dumping it on page three, and so forth.

You can only self-edit to your own skill level. This is why you need a second person to look over your work. A second person, whom you trust will be able to see things that you cannot, they will see what is on the page unclouded by the knowledge that you have about characters or plot. Yes, it is horrible to get feedback which says that a character you wrote is horrible or not understandable, or that your prose is muddy, or lacks description, or is drowning in description, but being a writer means hearing things we don't want to hear.

BETA READERS AND PROFESSIONAL HELP

Once you have drafted and edited your work to the stage where you feel comfortable sharing it with others, it is time to give your work to a friend to read and gain feedback. Make sure your friend knows that they will be interrogated by you before they start so that they can take notes as they read. If they are not willing to do this, find someone different because you need feedback that is more than "I liked it." or "I didn't like it." Also, make sure they read and like the genre, you write in.

Not all the feedback you will be given will be of use to you. You won't agree with all of it, you won't use all of it. But it is useful to see your work through another's eyes. Generally speaking though, if multiple people identify the same aspect of your manuscript as problematic, then chances are it is a problem and you would be well advised to address their concerns.

A word of caution, some readers can be extraordinarily uncharitable or down right toxic when giving feedback. These readers may be writers themselves and view your writing as a threat, subscribing to a belief that an opportunity given to another is an opportunity denied them. Or just jealous and mean people who delight in ripping others down. If a reader attacks your writing, or your right to call yourself a writer, or your self-worth, that is a person to avoid and to protect your writing from. If you find that it is hard to find honest charitable feedback in your social sphere, then it is best to have a professional read your work. It will cost a fee, but better to pay a fee than to pay with your self-esteem.

Eventually you will have to move away from friends and have your manuscript formally assessed. This is a paid service that helps you to identify structural weaknesses in a manuscript and sort them out before you send to a publisher or decide to self-publish. Professional help has a bit of a bad rap among unpublished writers. You see somewhere in the mists of time a writer had a very bad experience with an editor and this story has been passed down from generation to generation of writers as a warning against the nefarious designs of wicked editors. I think it also stems from the ideas that we absorb from school, where we learn that only people who get top marks are the winners and that any criticism of the work you produce makes you a failure. Having been on both sides of the equation, I can tell you that I don't have a pointed hat or winged monkeys when I am editing a writer's work. Nor does constructive criticism ever feel less cringe worthy than a full Brazilian.

SO WHY SHOULD YOU SUBMIT YOUR WORK TO A PROFESSIONAL EDIT?

Firstly let me explain that there are two types of editing: Structural and Copy editing.
A structural edit looks at your manuscript as a whole and helps you to identify weak spots, logical inconsistencies, clichés, potential copyright issues, redundancies in the plot, and ultimately helps you create a better reading experience. Basically it is like a mechanic looking at your engine and finding out why it is making that horrible banging noise. A good editor will not only diagnose what is causing the banging noise, they will also tell you that your exhaust is leaking and your fan belt is on its last legs. And they will work with you to help rectify the situation. Of course you may wish keep your work just as it is, as is your right. But, is it better to know there is a problem before publication, than to wonder down the track why your book isn't selling?

Copyediting is what people generally think of when they think of an edit. Copyediting tidies up your spelling, grammar, punctuation. This is the step that most people think that they can skip. Editors are interested in your work speaking as clearly as possible. Well edited prose flows and is a pleasure to read. Readers can tell the difference between edited and unedited prose and even free samples of unedited prose do not sell books. Readers do not want to have to guess at your meaning, they want it to be clear the first time, and editors help you create that.
Editing is NOT an optional extra that you can skip to keep the price of your self-published work down. Editing is the difference between writing a book that people want to read and one that they don't. You are a writer, writing is about communicating, editing helps you do that.

So you have finished your first draft of your manuscript. Congratulations take a break; give yourself a small reward, Belgian chocolate, a nice glass of wine, whatever works for you.
Now put your manuscript in a drawer for a week, don't look at it or think about it. You have been working on it intensely for some time and you and your manuscript need some time apart. After a week take your manuscript out of the drawer and read it again, considering what your intentions were when you started writing. Does this manuscript live up to those

intentions? If not does it offer a different path to take your story? Or can you see what needs to be changed to bring it back to your intentions? What further research needs to be undertaken to bring your story in line with your expectations.

Use your journal to workshop these thoughts.

TYPICAL ISSUES WITH 1ST DRAFTS.

- Too little or too much description- Both of these are a problem. Too little description and the scene looks as if it is occurring in a white box. Too much description and I cannot know what to focus on especially when lush prose is accompanied by no plot.
- Back story- I know that you think the reader must know all about the turbulent relationship the character had with her father so that we can understand her from the outset, but honestly, we don't. If I need to know that, make that what the book is about and show me that story. If it is something that I need to know to understand the character, give it to me in small doses the same way that you might learn something like that about a new friend. We are all very off put by people who give their whole life story in a first meeting, the opening of a book is no different. Don't over share.
- Be aware of repetition- Everyone repeats words and everyone has their own words that they repeat. Try to be aware of which words these are (mine is 'just' I use it far too often) and weed them out when you are reading over your draft.
- The overuse of adjectives and adverbs- Despite our best intentions these little suckers can slip in to our writing. Try and weed as many as you can out and watch as your writing instantly improves.

It is important to note that none of these problems are fatal. Writing is a bit like juggling a broken bottle, a flaming torch and a running chainsaw while being chased by a lion, you will drop some if not all of the techniques in your eagerness to get the story down at times. That is why first drafts are never shown to anyone.

Now it is time to work on your second draft using the experience of your first to help you improve it. This process is repeated until you have a manuscript you are willing to share with another person. Preferably find several people and compare and contrast their feedback, things that multiple people pick up on are problems that must be addressed ones that are noticed by singular readers can be addressed at your discretion. Make sure your friends know that they will be interrogated by you before they start so that they can take notes as they read. If they are not willing to do this, find someone else because you need feedback that is more than "I liked it." or "I didn't like it." Also, make sure they read and like the genre, you write in.

Once you have a manuscript which receives positive feedback from your friends, you can choose to have it professionally assessed by a manuscript assessor or to submit it to a publisher.

SENDING WORK OUT

Firstly, not everything that you write will be for a public audience. Everyone writes private works for family and friends only. There is nothing wrong with this in fact this is the audience that you use to develop your writing and your confidence to the point that you are ready to submit to commercial publications.

When you do submit to a publication or an agent or publisher, there are some important things to remember.

- Have realistic expectations – Publishing is a business not a charity. Publishers, from the smallest online journal to the largest international corporation are in business, they are interested in writing that they know will sell to their readers. If you have no name and no reputation, you need to build a publishing history; this means publishing lots of works in small journals for little or no payment. For most journals, a complimentary copy is given in payment.

- Humility goes a long way – when approaching an editor you must be confidant and promote your work, but not arrogant. The reality of the situation is that you are a tiny fish (not even that, you aspire to be a tiny fish). You are plankton, the tiny things that fish eat. So you are not in a position to argue the point with an editor or question their ability to judge or reject your work. It is not a good look. Confidence in your work is what you need to sell it, but rudeness is the quickest route to having your e-mail blocked by prospective editors for all time.

- This will take time – you will receive a huge number of rejection letters before you are accepted. If an editor gives you encouragement, invites you to submit again or comments positively on your work, take it as a positive. Editors are busy people and do not do this for everyone. Put them and

their journal at the top of your list next time round.
- **Subscribe to Journals** – You should subscribe to a few Literary Journals. This helps you to understand what is being published at this time. Also supporting the publications that support beginning and early career writers is good karma. Some journals read the submissions of subscribers before they will read others so it can pay to subscribe in the end.
- **You get paid** – if a publisher asks you to pay them in return for publishing your work don't accept. It doesn't mean your work is good, it means that they are a Vanity press. They will swallow your money, your 'book' will be unavailable in shops, buried online, and your wallet will never recoup its losses. Receiving a free copy is still payment, paying to appear in a journal is vanity publishing.
- **Write a good letter** – I am the editor of a small e-journal and I have yet to receive a properly written submission letter. Because I am small I am not picky about this yet, but I am an exception not the rule. When I send work out I write a proper submission letter and you should too. Because without one, your work will be rejected unread by prospective editors.

FINAL THOUGHTS

The publishing world is a business world and it is not an easy business to enter. If this is where you wish to go then you will need a bucket load of confidence and strong support from your family and friends. Creative writing is a rich and rewarding activity. Where you choose to take your writing is up to you, not everyone who writes, does so for a public audience and not every work even by published writers is written for public consumption. However, everyone who writes does so because they find it a richly rewarding activity. I hope that you enjoy your writing life regardless of where it takes you.

Week 12
   ◦ **40,000 -45,000 words. After the climax, how has the character changed? How has their world changed for the better or the worse? A final scene to provide closure to the reader.**

WRITING JOURNAL ACTIVITIES.

Choose an object that has some particular resonance for you personally. Contemplate the object; look deeply at it turning over all the details of it in your mind. Think about what it means to you and how it came into your life. In your journal, write a page approx 300 words about the object.

LOST SOULS ACTIVITY

Chose a picture of a person you don't know and write as much as possible about that person. Superficial details like job and home and wealth should be kept to a minimum, rather you should focus on the personality of the person.
    How do they see themselves?
    What are their close relationships like and why?
    - What are their spiritual beliefs?
    - What are their attitudes to:
- Sex.
- Divorce.
- Marriage.
- Adultery.
- Children.
- Their parents.
- Their siblings.
- The environment.
- Death.
- Their work.
- Their community.

    - What helped form these attitudes?

Take the character you created in the lost souls activity and write a short scene which shows one or more aspects of their personality and appearance. DO NOT write a mirror scene, i.e., She looked in the mirror and saw (insert whole character profile) and was unhappy with the image reflected back. This is an example of the poorest writing and should be avoided at all costs. Looking in the mirror should be a neutral or better still character developing act, not short hand for a lazy writer to dump character information on the reader. Try to show them doing something alone and use what you know about them to inform how they do the activity.

DIALOGUE PRACTICE: WHAT IS NOT BEING SAID?

Everyone has been in a situation where one person speaks and the other passive aggressively uses silence and body language to ignore and aggravate the other person. In order to practice the use of body language and silence in dialogue write a scene where one person talks and the other responds using body language and minor vocalisations, e.g. sighing.

CHARACTER BUILDING TEMPLATE

Character name:
Role in story: eg. protagonist, antagonist, secondary character, etc.

Physical appearance: Focus on what makes your character unique. Nobody remembers blonde hair and blue eyes, but they do remember a limp, or a scar, or hair that refuses to be styled.
What sort of first impression do they make? Is this accurate?

How do they act when they are alone?

What are their goals?

How do their goals conflict with others?

Who do they get along with well? What does that look like?

Who do they get along badly with? What does that look like?

How do they get in their own way?

How do they respond to setbacks?

How does their past dictate their current actions and behaviour?

How do their goals dictate their current actions and behaviour?

Where do you want your character to be by the end of the story? How have they grown? What is their arc?

RESEARCH TEMPLATE.

Source Type:
Source Title:
Source location: Web address, book etc.
Pertinent information:

How does this information relate to your story?

What new research does this information require?

How might the information impact the narrative/thesis of your work? What modifications might be necessary to incorporate this new research into your work?

HISTORICAL RESEARCH TEMPLATE.

Source Type: Primary/Secondary.
Source Title:
Source location: Web address, book etc.
Pertinent information:

How does this information relate to your story/history/memoir?

What new research does this information require?

How might the information impact the narrative/thesis of your work? What modifications might be necessary to incorporate this new research into your work?

TEMPLATE FOR BETA READER FEEDBACK.

Book title:
In your own words what is the book about?

What sort of first impression does it make?

What aspects of the book resonated with you?

What aspects of the book turned you off or hindered your reading experience?

What aspects of the narrative did you find confusing?

Which characters particularly resonated with you? Why?

Which characters did you find difficult to engage with? Why?

What aspects of the language interfered with your reading experience? Why?

Were there any plot issues that hindered your reading?

Based on the manuscript as it stands now, how likely would you be to recommend it to a friend to read? Why, why not?
What is the biggest takeaway that the author should know based on your reading experience?

SYNOPSIS WRITING TEMPLATE

What is your story about? (write ONE sentence. Focus on the main narrative.)

What is your story about? (write ONE paragraph. Focus on the main narrative. Briefly mention any subplots.)

What is your story about? (write ONE page. Each sentence in your paragraph should be expanded to a paragraph. Focus on the main narrative. Briefly mention any subplots.)

SUBMISSION LETTER/E-MAIL TEMPLATE

Your Name
Address
Telephone Number
Email

Editor/Agent's Name
Editor/Agent's Title
Name of organisation
Address of the organisation

Date

Dear ….(find out the name of the editor and address it to them it because if you don't know who they are why should they care who you are?),

(Name of the piece you have enclosed)

What is your piece about? (one – two paragraphs should suffice). Who your target audience is and why you think it would be a good fit for the publisher. Be sure to include if this is a simultaneous submission.
If you are an unpublished writer give any relevant background for your writing. If you are over 22 don't talk about High School English classes. Let the recipient know why you are the best possible writer for this work.
If you are an established writer or graduate, include a brief biography. It should be no longer than a paragraph.
Thank you for your time and consideration.
Sincerely,
(Your Name)

INDEX

A
ADJECTIVES, 53, 68-69, 83
ADVERBS, 53, 67-68, 72, 83
ANALEPSIS, 54, 55-56
ARCHETYPES, 24-25
ASTROLOGY, 21
AUSTIN, 16, 38
AUTHOR, 4, 9, 43, 47-48, 50, 55, 97

B
BEGIN, 8, 10, 30-31, 67, 80
BEGINNER, 10, 36, 72
BEGINNING, 7, 35, 41, 55, 74, 85
BRAINSTORMING, 21
BRONTE, 16, 63
BURROUGHS, 60

C
CHARACTER, 8, 15, 19, 21-22, 24-26, 30-32, 35, 37, 40-42, 54-55, 58, 64, 66-67, 69, 71-77, 80, 83, 87-90
CHEKOV, 55
COPYEDITING, 82

D
DESCRIPTION, 37, 43, 53, 71-73, 80, 83
DETAIL, 37, 42, 54, 75, 87
DIALOGUE, 71-74, 80, 88
DICKENS, 32
DISCOURSE, 76-77
DOSTOYEVSKY, 32
DRACULA, 60

E
EDIT, 12, 80, 82
EDITING, 23, 79-82
EDITOR, 66, 81-82, 84-85, 100

EMPATHY, 23
ENDINGS, 33
ETHICS, 62-64
EXTROVERT, 26

F
FEEDBACK, 80-81, 83-84, 95
FEMINIST, 48
FICTION, 15-17, 24, 28-29, 33, 35, 37-38, 40-42, 45, 47, 55, 59, 75
FICTOCRITICISM, 59
FLASHBACK, 54
FOCALISATION, 74
FORESHADOWING, 54-55

G
GENRE, 15-17, 23, 29, 35-36, 38, 40-42, 47, 59, 81, 84

H
HYPERTEXT, 59

I
IMAGERY, 68, 70

J
JOURNAL, 7-9, 16, 83-85, 87
JOYCE, 58

K
KAFKA, 58
KEATS, 60

L
LITERARY, 15-16, 35, 40-42, 47-49, 55, 58, 60, 71

M
MACBETH, 42
MARXIST, 47

MELVILLE, 32
METAFICTION, 51
METAPHORS, 70
MODERNISM, 49
MYTHOLOGY, 17, 21, 30

N
NARRATOR, 30, 50-51, 55, 58, 71, 73-77
NEWSPAPERS, 17
NOVELIST, 17-18, 25, 54, 59-60
NOVELS, 9, 11, 15-16, 24, 28-29, 31-32, 36, 38, 42, 48

P
PASTERNAK, 50
PICARESQUE, 28
PLANNING, 7, 10-12, 19
PLOT, 15, 17, 20, 24, 26, 28-30, 32, 35, 37-38, 40, 42, 54, 63, 67, 73, 80, 82-83, 97
POETRY, 70
POSTCOLONIAL, 49
POSTMODERN, 50-51
POSTMODERNISM, 49
POUND, 50
PROLEPSIS, 55-56
PROLOGUE, 37
PROSE, 29, 58, 60, 66, 70-71, 79-80, 82-83
PROSPECTIVE, 84-85
PROTAGONIST, 15, 36-38, 41, 72, 74-75, 77, 89
PSYCHOLOGICAL, 25, 42, 58
PUBLISHER, 4, 11, 16, 38, 59, 79, 81, 84-85, 100

R
READER,10, 15, 17, 21-23, 28-30, 33, 36-38, 41, 44, 48, 50-51, 53-54, 59-60, 66-75, 77, 81, 83, 88
RESEARCH, 4, 8, 15-17, 22, 64, 83, 91-94

S
SIMILES, 70

STORY, 7-8, 10, 12, 15-25, 28-30, 32-33, 35-36, 38, 40-42, 44, 47, 49, 53-56, 58, 62-64, 66-68, 71-76, 80-81, 83, 89-91, 93, 98-99
STORYBOARD, 20
STORYTELLING, 23-24, 42
SUBMISSION, 85, 100
SURREALISM, 58
SYNOPSIS, 98

T
TEMPLATE, 89, 91, 93, 95, 98, 100

V
VERBS, 68, 70
VOICE, 50, 55, 69-71, 76-77

W
WOOLF, 50, 58

ABOUT THE AUTHOR

Natalie Muller is a writer, teacher and founder of Black Cockie Press and The Wild Goose Literary e-Journal, an e-Journal for new Australian writing. She holds a Master of Arts in Writing from Swinburne University of Technology. She has taught Creative Writing through WEA Sydney and privately. From 2014 -2019 Natalie developed, piloted and implemented the Editor- in-Residence program with the BMCC Library.
Poisoning the Nest her first novel is also published by Black Cockie Press.

www.ingramcontent.com/pod-product-compliance
Lightning Source LLC
Chambersburg PA
CBHW060522010526
44107CB00060B/2656